Home Care
Business Marketing

Jane John-Nwankwo RN

ISBN-13: 978-1494860370

ISBN-10: 1494860376

DEDICATION

Dedicated all new home care agency owners.

The Home Health Aide Textbook

Home Care Principles

Jane John-Nwankwo
RN, MSN

HOW TO MAKE A
MILLION IN NURSING

The First Five Steps

Jane John-Nwankwo
RN, MSN

"It does not matter the quality of products you have, what matters is if you have clients"

Jane John-Nwankwo RN, MSN

Have you bought these books?

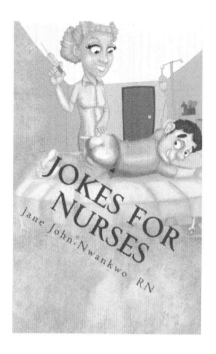

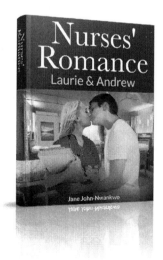

1 CHAPTER ONE

An Overview Of How To Market A Home Care Business

A home care business is gaining a lot of prominence today as not only does it provide one with a regular cash inflow it also is a noble venture to enter into. In the United States of America today, there are a good number of individuals entering into the home care industry to serve the elderly and the disabled. This sector is a booming sector and is rising steadily. It is lucrative business but at the same time very challenging. Catering to the elderly and disabled requires a lot of patience and compassion. If one does not have a genuine love for social service, he should not enter into this profession merely for earning profits. The home care business venture requires one to be strong and patient for he needs to tackle people who cannot carry out their lives in a normal manner. These people are totally dependent on home care professionals and as a result the home care giver must be a person who is sensitive to their needs.

At the outset, the first step that should be taken by a person who is interested in entering into this venture is the market. Every business targets a segmented market. A detailed survey must be undertaken by the person. Understanding the marketing demands will help him into the venture. Planning and implementation of strategies are directly related. Without the right business acumen the venture may fail to be successful. The home care business deals with both medical and non-medical facilities. The first and foremost thing that the person must do is acquire professional home care training. Being a licensed and certified home care professional will assure people to depend on you. The elderly or disabled person is a loved one that requires special care. The family members or the relatives of the patient cannot afford to put the responsibility of their special one in wrong hands. The certification and professional training will induce them to rely on you and promote subsequent word of mouth successfully.

It is difficult for a sole individual to administer and monitor everything in a business. There needs to be decentralization and thus a sharing of responsibilities. The same goes for any home care business. The person who intends to start the business should not only be qualified but he needs to recruit the right people to aid him in this noble venture. Hiring the right personnel is important. Not only does he need to take into consideration their qualifications but he has to check on their interpersonal skills as well. The home care business deals with patients who are cranky and suffer from loss of memory. They may be difficult to handle and at times may cause tantrums. This is turn may result in a normal person losing patience with the patient. A home care giver must be sensitive, understanding, compassionate and loving. He or she must have a patient oriented attitude and medical expertise to handle emergencies. The home care giver becomes an integral part of the patient's life as there is a major degree of dependence by both the patient and his or her family members.

Recruiting professionals for the home care business must be done with time and caution. All the staff should be trained and medically updated with patient needs as and when required. These professionals should be friendly and sensitive to the patient and they must have a good presence of mind to handle urgencies calmly. The home care giver along with his team makes a difference to the patient's life. In fact they are more of friends and thus are blindly relied upon by many families in the United States today.

As mentioned above, the home care business venture requires elaborate and detailed survey. Depending on this, the marketing strategies should be chalked out. The location of the venture plays an important role in reaching out to the maximum number of clients successfully. The growing statistics are very encouraging in the country and the demand for home care professionals are consistently on the rise. Since the business is a full time service it helps to reap in handsome profits to the owner. This business covers both medical and non-medical services that cater to patients. For those interested for home care business ventures they must be prepared for intense traveling and negotiations with a number of people. The aspiration to bring a difference to the lives of many patients should drive them to set up a booming home care unit with good credentials. The quality and the integrity of the home care unit will play a vital role in drawing customers to the person.

Once the market trends have been determined the person must

get a license for setting up the venture. The State provides the license and in case the State demands any specific fees, one should pay them to the authorities concerned. Another significant step that should be taken by the person is the preparation of a business plan that should contain the description of the strategies and prices. The focus of the person should be the building of contacts and networking skills here are of utmost importance. Positive word of mouth helps every business in a huge way. Be it a sole proprietorship, partnership, limited liability Company, S Corporation and C Corporation, the company needs to be registered with the Secretary of The State. One needs to also obtain the Federal Employer Identification Number (EIN) from the IRS. This coupled with a private home care business plan can help the person immensely in initiating, operating and expanding the business.

In the United States of America, people who are interested in home care business ventures must get the necessary licenses, registrations and insurance for the business. The City or County license is also very essential and hence the person should apply for them too. In some States of the USA, a person needs to get the Sales Tax License number too. There are 23 States in the country that also require as a home care license for non-medical homecare services. The other necessities include the registration which the State Revenue Department. There are some States that allow applicants to register online. Registration with the State Employment Service is mandatory along with the purchase of the workers insurance compensation and business liability insurance, fire insurance on office, valuable papers and other associated items. This is not compulsory for those who take up offices, they are equally important for those who have set up home care units at home too.

A good home care unit also boosts of a successful office system that includes the employee records, the scheduling process, the payroll process, billing and collection and the intake procedure. There should also be a good policy for the retention of employees of the home care unit. For those who are into a home care business that is based at home, they have the option of framing their own business policies. Along with this there should be the careful planning and execution of a successful sales and marketing strategy that should be specifically designed to meet one's business needs in mind.

Once the above has been taken care of the next step that the person should do is decide on what marketing tools are required to spread awareness about one's home care services with success. The marketing tools are very crucial for the growth of the business and the attraction of clients. The home care business can provide some additional services like home based physical therapy, counseling, nutritionist services and even alternate therapy like acupuncture. The concentration on additional services can thus enhance a positive word of mouth and increase patronage among customers with ease.

In the Unites States of America, insurance plans also play a vital role in determining the growth of the home based business. There are many people who can get the services of a home care business only on the acceptance of insurance plans. It is prudent for the home based unit to accept as many insurance plans in order to increase the client base. The home care business should keep an understanding and sensitive insurance counselor who can advise prospective patients and relatives on the types of insurance plans that are available in the market. He can play a vital role in making them understanding the positive and the negative points of the insurance plans. The home care business can also keep a professional insurance advisor who can advise the person on the benefits and limitations of the insurance plan. If there are any modifications in the plan, the insurance advisor can also advise them accordingly. In this way customer satisfaction can be enhanced.

Another positive manner in which one can enhance one business is by entering into agreements with clinic and hospitals for additional medical facilities. In this manner both can get good profits from the venture. The level of care that is given to each patient generally depends on the condition. The transfer to another medical facility may be required and these agreements are very useful. Not only are the patients benefited but the home care unit also gets many client referrals too. These client referrals can help enhance the business in a very encouraging and positive manner easily.

The above agreements are generally framed and crafted in great detail. There are other agreements that the home care unit may enter into and these are for expert services. In such agreements the home care unit should pay a small contractual fee that is mutually decided by both the parties. These professional agreements create a strong bond and when clients come to the home care unit for services they too are convinced that their loved one is in safe hands. In additional to the above the home care unit can also enter into other basic community services like monitoring blood pressure, blood sugar, etc. This helps the local people be aware of the home care center and thus helps the business to grow in many ways that one.

In order to promote and project the above mentioned services the home care unit has to take up advertising modes. There are many advertising modes that a company can resort to for the purpose of projecting the image of the company. For local marketing fliers are the best means to highlight the services of the company to the public. The best places to distribute these fliers are hospitals, churches, shopping centers and in the neighborhood. The use of business cards is also very helpful for the promotion of the business as they can be carried easily and handed out to any person whenever required. These business cards are also very helpful to project a very professional image.

The internet is a very good advertising medium and also much cost effective. The home care unit can make its own website and include vital details on it. The person can include write ups and articles on home care and its related articles. One can also include the press releases on the site. Very often these press releases can be picked up by news feed and hence increase the traffic flow to the site. There are also email marketing tools that the home care can also adopt for the purpose of marketing. Visitors can see the website and contact one through this platform. Moreover, the internet does not have any geographical limitations and can reach out to a large number of persons.

Another effective medium is the radio. This audio advertising medium can spread the message of the home care unit to many clients. The home care units can also provide information in the form of radio programs where the unit can spread home care education to a wide number of listeners in the country. For this venture many people can come to know about the senior elderly care, family relationships, aging, health, nutrition, childcare, long term insurance and caring etc.

The print media is also very helpful and customer oriented. The home care unit can also place advertisements in newspapers and magazines to project the services of the home care center. For those who can invest more, billboards and hoardings are also very effective. They should be positioned in prominent locations. The graphics and the text must be compelling in order to make an impact on the people who see and read them.

There are other marketing strategies that the home care business can refer to for the promotion of one's business. The person can adopt any one or all of the advertising tools that have been mentioned above. The person needs to keep track of the changing marketing scenario and as per the situation adopt the right marketing tool. The market has to be watched and the advertising tool should be varied in order to meet the changing demands. These tools can be used best with market research and survey.

From the above, it is evident that the right marketing strategy and its relative advertising tools can go a long way in enhancing the image of the company. Along with the external marketing tools, the professionals who are associated with the home care unit must have a friendly and customer oriented attitude. This provides the much needed personal touch which can make a huge difference in enhancing the goodwill and reputation of the unit. The higher the goodwill, the more client referrals come in and hence there is larger business. The home care unit can provide both live in assistance and home visits. The members should be compassionate individuals and they must love doing service to the elderly and the disabled.

The home care service can also focus on providing other social beneficial services like errand running, lawn care services, financial planning, pet care services, food delivery and preparation, home cleaning etc. This service can be provided by the unit or it can be done with the partnership of another agency. The revenue can be shared by both and this is a very popular venture for getting extra income. These partnerships are done on a contractual basis and they are helpful to get extra income.

The home care business is growing and is ideal for those who have a passion for social service and love for human beings. The home care business is a very noble and honorable profession. In order to join this profession one does not have to be of a certain age. Anyone who is interested in providing love and care to people can successfully turn this passion into a lucrative business. The home care industry is fast growing and there are many people who are depending on these services for providing care and love to patients. The business is booming today and with planning can be made into a very profitable one. There are many sources and avenues to earn extra money. The home care business is such a venture that gives you both a decent income and respect from all walks of life.

2 CHAPTER TWO

Homecare is defined as a variety of community based services that help in supporting somebody who is recovering from an acute condition like a hip fracture or services required by individuals suffering with chronic conditions like cerebral palsy or stroke. The duties as well as skills of home personnel differ from the other; however, despite this fact they have one thing in common! What? Well, they take adequate care of the patients and ensure that they are living in a safe environment. This isn't all; they also offer family caregivers an opportunity to refill their depleted emotional as well as physical reserves.

Homecare personnel comprises of:

• **Registered nurses (RNs)** — they provide expertise medical care, including offering medications, dressing wounds, monitoring significant wounds, as well as teaching family caregivers the ways of using complicated tools at home.

• **Therapists** — they help patients in restoring as well as maintaining their speech, motor as well as cognitive skills.

• **Homecare aides**—they offer personal services like dressing, bathing, making meals, toileting, and light cleaning, as well as taking patients to the medical health practitioner.

• **Companion/homemakers**—they help with chores around the house however do not carry out personal duties for the patient.

So if you want to step into a home care business then you first step involves in recruiting the aforementioned personnel!

Once you have recruited the personnel, the next step that would help you out in marketing your home care business is through your offered services. Now, your offered services should be something like:

- The first step involves in ensuring that your group of personnel are effective in handling the patients. To be more specific, when in their company the patients should not feel that they are away from home.
- You need to define the tasks that requite to be performed by the homecare worker. For instance, recruit a nurse who would clean as well as bandage the wounds of the patient and keep a check on his/her health condition as well. Or rather let's say that you need to appoint home care personnel who would help the patient in dressing them up as well as bathing them and much more.

- Make sure to market your home care business by setting a reasonable price for your services offered. This will allow more and more people to grab the services offered by you.

Many people get confused when it comes choosing a homecare solution. In other words, they are in hunt of some homecare solution that offers services at a reasonable price. So for marketing your homecare business effectively, make sure to offer your services at a reasonable price that seems affordable to the general mass.

Home care agencies may be referred to as the companies that are there to cater to the homecare requirements. However, each and every home care agencies doesn't offer the same level and variety of service, hence, make sure that the agency you want to go for helps you out with the needed services.

So if you are interested to start your home care business and market it simultaneously, then let me tell you that this article is sure to help you out. So here we go...

Healthcare is a rapidly growing industry, thanks to the increase in life expectancies as well as aging population. Over the past century, the percentage of life expectancy has almost doubled. As a result, the need for home care services is increasing at a raging speed. This isn't all, people who are recuperating from surgeries, illnesses, or injuries also need to opt for the services of home care business. So friends, by now you must have come to know the importance of starting off with your personal home care business.

When you initially start off with a home care business, you need to interact with individuals who require help carrying out basic duties such as feeding themselves, housecleaning as well as bathing. Make sure that the person you choose are compassionate and caring. However, prior to starting off with marketing your home care business, make sure you have the following skills in you:

- Medical experience
- Capable of understanding medical terminology as well as relaying doctor's orders to patients
- Capable for teaching patients the ways through which they can adjust to their illness or injury and how to take adequate care of their own selves.
- Capable of addressing the needs of the patients as well as their family members.
- Capable of reading doctors' orders as well as executing them appropriately.

The benefits that come with owing a home care business are as follows:

- You can work at your own pace...that means you are your own boss
- You can perform a reliable service to the community
- You can market your services in an effective manner
- The payment plan is satisfactory

- You have in your hand the option of purchasing a franchise that helps with supplies, insurance, licenses and much more

You can market your agency effectively only if it is certified and accredited. Some of the recognized organizations are the Joint Committee for Accreditation of Healthcare Organizations, the National League for Nursing, and the National Foundation of Hospice and Home Care. Once certified, your home care business is at par with the national industry standards.

Now, in addition to effective marketing, you need to also take into consideration the fees that you are supposed to charge from the patient. In general, agencies charge fees that are anything in between $100 to $120 per visit. On the flip side, there are some home care agencies that charge the fees on hourly basis. Whatever fees you may charge, make sure that it is reasonable as this approach helps in the effective marketing of your home care business.

Starting as well as managing a home care business needs talent and motivation. As mentioned earlier, as soon as you start off with your business, your next step involves in marketing it. However, before you take up any step you need to do a good research work and plan your things accordingly. Devote ample time, before exploring as well as evaluating your personal and business goals. Next, you need to use this detail for creating a comprehensive as well as thoughtful business plan which helps you to acquire your goal- your dream of marketing your home care business successfully.

Check out the keys to market your home care business effectively:

- You need to first start off with the reasons for which you want to move into this business. In general, there are a couple of reasons for which people opt for this business. These are as follows:
  1. financial independence
  2. self-management
  3. creative freedom
  4. full use of knowledge and personal skills

Towards, the beginning of the article, the personnel that you need to recruit for carrying out your home care business has been mentioned clearly to you. It is only when you hire good employees that you can market your business all the more effectively. Make sure that the employees you choose don't have a past record of criminal abuse and activity. You can find relevant details as well as source from employees with the help of a home care registry. These registries are somewhat same as the employment agency. Many counties and states provide homecare services to disabled and aged people. Some also offer services to family caregivers.

You must be surprised to know that home care business is a flourishing one and has acquired much fame in the United States. There are nearly 30,000 providers in the United States that provide both medical services as well as non-medical services. So friends, you can very well guess the cut throat competition that you are going to come across. Hence, make sure market your business well!

Nearly ten million people and even more are in need of this service because they either suffer from certain health conditions or are aged and need adequate care at home. The yearly expenses for personal care that is associated with health issues as well as old age in the United States amount to nearly billions of dollars.

Another marketing tool is your target audience or in other words, before marketing your business, you need to find out who requires home care business. To begin with, there are millions and millions of people who are ill and need adequate care at home. People who have sufficient money are free to sign up with the services of home care business. Second, with the increase in the elderly population, the need for non-medical care services is increasing at a raging speed in recent times. It is because; most of them prefer living in their own homes rather than moving into old age homes. In a nutshell, home care is a broad term that takes into account a varied collection of services related to health. Make sure that the services you promote help in restoring your well-being as well as health.

That's fine, right now you may be busy with your marketing venture, but in a fit to do so, please don't overlook the needs as well as desires of your clients. Instead you need to devote some time in finding out what your clients really want. In case of non-medical home care clients, the motivations lie in taking care of elderly as well as sick people. It is much simple to jot down your services in pen and paper, but it is much challenging to turn these services into a reality.

So, when you walk up to a client there's point in simply explaining your services, instead try discussing with them the reasons behind offering these services.

Successful home care companies offer compassionate care which keeps patients' loads as well as profits high. Whether your business concentrates on live in assistance or short term visits your company is sure to increase its profit margin as well as clientele with the help of a well-structured marketing plan. The most efficient marketing ideas for home care engage in offering adequate car, reliable complementary services as well as well formed visibility amongst medical facilities and probable home care clientele.

Following is a list of marketing ideas that would help you in carrying out your marketing venture successfully. Check them out…

- Don't restrict your services to one. Provide a variety of services to your prospective clients. In addition to nursing care, you can provide other services such as:
    1. at-home physical therapy
    2. nutritionist services
    3. counseling
    4. even alternative therapies such as acupuncture

This choice allows customers to concentrate on their health care more adequately. In addition to this, it paves your way to offer more comprehensive care to your clients there helping you to earn good profits in the process. Well, this isn't all; you can also allure plenty of customers if you have at your hand variety of services from where they can make a selection.

Insurance is yet another marketing idea that is sure to help you out. Most patients get access to the home care facilities with the help of their insurance plan. So you can now enhance your prospective customer base by taking into consideration as many insurance plans as you can. In addition to this, you can also provide insurance consultations to your clients and help them in understanding their limitations as well as benefits. When suitable, ensure referring your clients to a screened insurance representative so that he or she can help by making the needed modifications to their already existing plan. You can also provide additional insurance for meeting the requirements of the patients. For avoiding the negative reactions of patients, ensure that the insurance sales representative you choose is extremely sensitive and offers options rather than providing sales hype. By maximizing the insurance benefits the home care patient can increase the revenue of your company.

Stay in touch with medical facilities such as nursing homes, hospitals, diabetes clinics hospice services, as well as other medical facilities which cater to the needs of elderly people as well as patients suffering with chronic conditions. In case of many patients, the level of care needed changes as soon as their condition progresses or improves. Developing a provider agreement together with other facilities may help patients in transferring between services and may lead to significant referrals for your services.

Ensure taking your home care business to an increasing number of public facilities for increasing awareness of your services and company. For instance, you need to offer basic care services such as blood pressure monitoring blood sugar checks, and flu shot services at any senior activity center. Apart from offering a convenient service, your company will show a friendly face for prospective clients. Allowing somebody to step into their home for providing care is much simpler fir people when they feel a bond to the providers.

In addition to the standard medical care required by home care patients, make sure to provide other beneficial services such as pet care services, home cleaning, financial planning, errand running, food delivery and preparation, and lawn care services. Sign up with partnership with individuals or companies who offer these services on contract basis which can tailor their services to home care patient's requirements. Apart from increasing the business of the partner company, you may request a finder's revenue or fee which increases your profit margin. In addition to offering additional income to your company, you need to offer easier access to required services for home care patients.

Marketing isn't directly related to technology. Don't believe my words? Well, try consulting the good communicators and they are sure to give you the same reply that technology is subject to change. If you think that you are not good at marketing, then you are free to hire a good marketer. Appropriate marketing always finds a way following which it will spread. All you need to do is get ahead of the other marketing giants as this is the ideal way through which you can market your home care business effectively. You can also create your personal website through which you can make people acquainted with the services you have in store for them. If you're independent you've the power to alter your website as well as your marketing strategy instantaneously.

As a home care business entrepreneur, make sure to take a look at the below mentioned opportunities:

- Arrange for business cards: that's true you can exchange business cards with other business professionals. In recent times, more and more people are eyeing on digital business cards as well as web based card exchange services.
- Setting up a home care business, isn't your sole priority, instead you need to make your business a reputed one. With adequate reputation, you are sure to get more and more clients at your doorstep.

So friends, why look for options, just go through these marketing ideas and take your home care business to the zenith of success!

3 CHAPTER THREE

There are many people in this world like the disabled and the elderly who do not have the ability to live like normal individuals. They suffer from some kind of health condition or terminal illness that does not permit them to perform their daily activities properly.

For those who are interested to help the likes of the above, starting a home care venture can give them a feeling of self-worth as well as make the lives of these elderly and disabled people more meaningful with their love. It also should be remembered that a Home Care Business is a venture that is not very easy. It is immensely challenging with difficulties, but highly rewarding for the person who undertakes the venture. For those who are interested in making a difference to the lives of millions of disabled and elderly people, opting for a home care business is a very wise choice. Every home care business provides companionship, personal care and professional nursing care.

The home care business in the country is growing as statistics show a marked increase in their demand. The home care service that is provided by businesses involve a full time service and hence provides a constant source of revenue to the owner of the home care business. The home care businesses offer both medical and non-medical services. A home care business gives the person the satisfaction of making a difference to the lives of thousands of people and brings a smile to their faces. For running a successful home care business, one requires to travel around often and meet a number of people. It is here that one should be using skills and well as some nursing knowledge that can enhance the quality and make the lives of the disabled and elderly people much better.

In order to begin with a home care business, one should first study the market trends in the health care industry. The next step is to get the license for the business and most states in the country require the applicant to produce a license that is properly filed by the State. This requires the applicant to fill up an application and submitting the specific fees to the State. Another thing that an applicant must do is design a business plan that should determine the target market along with the prices and strategies that need to be adopted. The next step that a person needs to keep in mind is building contacts and networking. No business can run without this vital feature as once ready to start one needs clients who will spread the word of mouth around to the others. In this case it is wise to consult a CPA or an advocate for advice.

The next step that one should take into account when starting a home business venture is the business name for the projection of the business in future. The venture that one can enter into may be in the nature of a sole proprietorship, partnership, limited liability company, S Corporation and C corporation. The company needs to be registered with the Secretary of The State and one need to also obtain the Federal Employer Identification Number (EIN) from the IRS. One should also set up the financial systems of the company and also open a business savings account for the operational costs of the venture. One should also draw up a private duty home care business plan that will help him or her in starting, operating and enhance the business.

In context to the above, a person should also get the required licenses, registrations and insurance for the business venture. One should also get a City or County license and if the State makes it compulsory one should get the Sales Tax License too. In the USA, there are 23 states that also require a home care license for non- medical home care companies. For any home care business, one must register with the State Revenue Department and in certain States one can also register online. A registration with the State Unemployment Service is also mandatory. One also needs to purchase the workers insurance compensation and business liability insurance. For any business venture, one also is required to purchase fire insurance on office, valuable papers and other related items. This is also required for those who have planned the home care business in their homes also.

A home care business also requires the setting up of office systems that also cover the intake and scheduling process, employee records, the payroll process along with the billing and the collection process. In the case of a home care business you have the option of framing your own individual policies and procedures or buying a policy or procedure manual. Every person also needs to develop and put into effect a successful care giver plan that deals with recruitment and retention of employees. There also should be the development of a good marketing and sales strategy that should be designed keeping the targets of one's business in mind.

One should recruit and hire one's business staff and then begin the process of building business relationships in the community. These solid business relationships can be established within the offices of doctors, nursing homes, small businesses, assisted livings and the non profits that offer service to the senior market. In order to function well internally one should also have a computerized scheduling and the billing system. The business should also offer ancillary services like emergency response systems and the setting up of an employee referral program so that the care givers that are presently employed in the business can help one with recruiting more caregivers as and when the need arises.

The most important aspect of the home care business venture is the investment in the sales and marketing that should bring in client inquiries and referrals. One has the option of joining the National Private Duty Association that is the sole national trade association that has been set up for the purpose of non medical home care companies. One should also needs the basic medical training that will give one the ability to care effectively for the needs of the disabled and elderly. Proper training with respect to administering medicine, changing dressings, feeding and preparing patients etc has to be exercised. One also needs to bathe the patients. Dealing with such patients can be hard at times as they are cranky and may also have suffered from memory loss. These patients require people that have extreme patience and gentle care. Professional certification is very essential for these people and in one's endeavor to help them.

One should also enter into connections with hospitals, nursing homes, diabetes clinic, or other medical facilities that provide services to patients and elderly with chronic ailments. The level of the care that is required by patients changes with the condition of the patient. The agreements should be well framed and hence clear to both the parties. This results in the creation of important referrals to the home care business. The home care business should also enter into a professional agreement with suppliers of health care services like, for example, a respiratory therapy provides in order to provide clinical support to the business. The range of clinical services usually includes respiratory or infusion therapy, nursing services, education and the instruction of the patient etc. The home care business usually pays a specific fee for these services. The home care business also should enter into advisor agreements in order to get expert services for the venture.

These professional agreements do not have any kind of legal concerns if they are structured and framed properly. The main concern of the preferred provider is to seek assurances that are primarily related to quality, accessibility and accountability.

They have to be implemented properly as these agreements contribute in establishing a long standing relationship that can be mutually beneficial to both parties.

The marketing of the home care business is a significant and important aspect of the business that needs to be minutely looked into. The advertising options that one can take up can range between the very cheap options like distributing fliers to the very expensive options like advertising in the newspaper. For effective local marketing, the distribution of fliers is a very simple and successful way to establish visibility in the community. The use of fliers is a simple and effective means to promote your business and the best places to distribute them are hospitals, churches, shopping centers and in the neighborhood. The use of business cards is also very effective and hence is a very successful marketing tool that also helps you get a professional image. They should always be kept in hand as there is no guarantee when a business opportunity may come in handy. When one hands them over to business clients, his network increases as these clients also promote business by referring potential clients too.

One can also market the home care business on the internet and build contacts on the net. One can create a web site for the company and project it on the website. The website of course should be designed by a professional and hence should contain vital links and information for the clients as well as visitors. One can also add one's business to an online directory for the purpose of expansion. One can promote one's home care business online by writing articles and press releases. If a good press release is picked up by a news feed the number of phone calls to the business will increase and hence contribute to spread awareness. There are also other associated tools like email marketing campaigns that can promote the business to a considerable extent. This results in the inflow of visitors and hence one can get business from a single platform.

The home care business can also opt for radio exposure. One can host a radio program on a monthly basis to reach out to a broader target audience. The home care business can address all kinds and types of home care services. There may be programs in which the home care business provider is featured in a guest show thus helping to spread the importance and awareness of the business to the targeted segment. Such programs also focus on very important home care services that cover senior elderly care, family relationships, aging, health, nutrition, childcare, long term insurance and caring etc.

One can also place advertisements in the newspapers and magazines to reach out to people. One should advertise in small publications like penny savers, community newspapers and area newsletters. They can also use billboards and hoardings at prominent places to project the image of the home care business. These can be put up in prominent places in order to attract the public and spread their image. One can also set up a booth at local health fairs, markets and community sales.

The marketing strategies to promote the home care business

are many and one just needs to think about the target audience. The main focus of marketing is not to sell the services. The main focus of these strategies is to create awareness, generate the need and then sell the product. One can also set up a referral program in which one can offer discounted rates to a person. One should be patient and make sure that he or she resorts to consistent marketing efforts to promote the business. One can change or adopt the different modes of advertising to get the maximum results with ease.

The home care businesses also focus on short term visits and live in assistance. As mentioned above the marketing plan has to be well crafted in order to get the maximum returns. The plan must focus on the key areas of enhancing complimentary services, a good potential home care medical facility etc. In order to get the maximum exposure for one's business one needs to offer a multitude of home care services for all the clients. In addition to providing the standard online nursing services one should also offer physical therapy, counseling, nutritional services and other alternative therapies like acupuncture. In order to draw more customers to one's home care business, it is prudent to offer additional services with the basic services.

In the USA, the access to home care services also depends upon the acceptance of insurance plans. In order to increase the customer base of the business one should be accept as many insurance plans as possible. One should offer insurance plans to the customers and provide consultation services to clients so that they may fully understand the terms and the conditions of the plans. The customers can also be aware of the benefits and the shortcomings of the various plans. When they have finally understood the terms and conditions, one should refer them to a professional insurance representative who can offer valuable advice with regard to the modifications in the existing plan. One should select a patient and claim insurance representative as patients may be difficult and the latter may lose patience. This will result in preventing negative customer reactions and can contribute to the maximization of the insurance benefits. This benefits both the home care business and the clients who come to them for their services.

The home care business can also benefit with the help of public care facilities in which the former can provide more public care services to the clients. Some of the most basic public care services that a home care business provides are blood sugar checks, blood pressure checks, flu shot services etc. In this manner the home care business will be happy to enhance its goodwill and prevent a friendly face to potential clients. Another popular marketing tool that can be provided by the home care business are the offering of other beneficial services like errand running, lawn care services, financial planning, pet care services, food delivery and preparation, home cleaning etc. These services can be provided by the home based businesses or they can partner with professional services on a contract basis. In such cases, one is also helping the partnered agency to earn profits too. One can also charge a revenue share that will increase profits and in addition to providing additional income to the business, they also provide one with easier access to the basic services for home care patients.

A home care business is noble venture that can be very profitable and rake in potential earnings per month. This is a booming business and it is fast evolving in the country today. The home care business is of immense help to those who need access to these professional services for their loved ones. They offer professional help, love and compassion and are trusted and relied upon by many families all over the country, Entering into home care business not only makes one earn decently, but also provide the much needed care services for those who need access to them with ease.

4 CHAPTER FOUR

. Broadly speaking, there are two kinds of home care providers and the skill needed for one differs from the other. The first kind of home care service is one that concentrates on helping people in carrying out their day to day tasks like cleaning, cooking, errands as well as personal hygiene. The second kind of home care service may help you in carrying out the day to day chores in addition to providing medication administration and in rare cases therapy.

There are quite a few options when it comes to starting off with a home care business. In fact, it can be rightly termed that the homecare business is flourishing at a raging speed. Why? Well, there are tow viable reasons behind the successful accomplishment of this industry namely:

- The aging population
- The desire to stay at home as people start aging

While the strength of people amongst the age group of 65 has increased to a considerable extent, in the like manner the life expectancy has almost double in the past century. It is estimated that people belonging to this age group will continue this upward growth curve quicker than any other age group.

This increase in growth has led to the need for compassionate as well as experienced home care services for the elderly people. In present years, innumerable people have turned out to be good business owners in the home care business. There are some people who have started their personal independent businesses, while there are some who have chosen to get into partnership with a skilled franchisor.

Can you guess who an ideal home care business owner is? Well, to begin with an interested party should first determine whether this business is suitable for you or not. To be more specific, an applicant should possess entrepreneurial spirit as well as should be willing to take the plunge.

Home care business owners should be compassionate and need to have a strong desire for offering valuable care services to their communities. Apart from compassion, experience also plays a viable role. You need to take in the risk factor if you are into any business venture. In addition to this, true entrepreneurs have an inborn sense of well calculated vs. inferior calculated risks. Though having a medical experience is not mandatory yet having one is certainly an added advantage. In fact, it is often observed that people with marketing and sales background often fare well in this sphere.

Signing up with a partnership with an experienced franchisor in the home care business brings with a lot of benefits when compared with an independent business. In other words, it allows a business owner to tap into a proven system. Franchisors provide structure for enabling business owners for attaining quick success, through ongoing support, training, sharing of information as well as industrial alliances. For instance, rather than looking for liability as well as worker's compensation insurance, a franchisor will offer preferred vendors with whom discounts can be negotiated.

There are states where a home health license or a home care license is needed; a renowned franchisor needs to offer significant assistance with the licensure and application process, down to writing agencies procedures and policies. On the other hand, independent business owner need to conduct their personal research into regulations for assuring compliance as well as avoiding fines or similar penalties.

Franchisors coordinate as well as hold national and regional meetings and frequent conference calls for disseminating information. Franchisors also provide management and marketing expertise, operational support together with the development of forms, public relations and branding.

The experienced franchisors help the franchisee to navigate through business set up, licensing, necessary software, insurance, caregiver recruitment and worker's compensation for enabling franchisees to concentrate on the most significant aspect of their business: generating revenue and acquiring clients.

There are some business owners who prefer doing things their personal way, without following a system. In general, these business owners prefer carrying out anything starting from branding, developing marketing collateral as well as establishing policy as well as procedures on their own as well as answer only to themselves.

In addition to this, the independent business owner can prefer developing local name recognition, vs. taking on a national persona as well as becoming the local representative. People who have worked in the senior care and home care community, referral sources, marketing contacts, and procedures and policies can already be established as well as partnering with a franchisor may appear unnecessary.

However, with the freedom and flexibility of independent ownership requires to be balanced together with the risks.

Before you market your home care business, you need to look for certain things in a franchise organization:

> Make sure to pay a personal visit together with corporate staff. Don't forget that you will have to work with these people, hence make sure that you share a good compatibility ratio.

The decision to partner with a franchisor or do it alone is solely your decision. Both these options have there are equal share of pros and cons. Hence prior to make any decision be sure that you weigh them both.

Ensure consulting with other home care business owners who have their independent business as well as those who have signed up with a franchise organization. The key lies in being satisfied with your business venture, hence prefer lots of questions and collect information before you make any important decision.

The bottom line is that if you want to start your own home care business, then your first step lies in learning about the market for senior services. Once your business is booming ensure coming back for additional tools as well as resources designed for helping you market, advertise as well as sell to seniors both offline and online.

Following, is a list of ideas that will help you start off as well as market your business effectively.

If you are planning to start your own home care business, then I must say that it's a wonderful decision. The elderly population is one amongst the rapidly growing segments and with it the demand for home care services is soaring. This implies that if you want to start off with a home care business, then there's a load of opportunity waiting on your way. Now you can make your dream of opening a home care business come true. So don't miss out on the opportunity to start off with this venture.

In order to market your home care business effectively, make sure that your business has the following provisions:

- Stay in constant touch with the patients so that they feel that there are people to care for them and look after them
- Carry out small errands such as visiting the post office, pharmacy, paying bills as well grocery shop on their behalf
- You can take them around and help them with some errands
- Carry out certain light cleaning on their part if they are unable to do so on their own (for example taking down drapes and cleaning, dusting or vacuuming in high or difficult to reach areas).

In addition to those mentioned above, you can also help them with various other services. The more services you provide, the more are the chances of people gaining familiarity with your home care business.

Have you ever wondered the ways through which you can market your home care business and that too without having to spare a penny on your part? If not, then take a look at the ways through which you can enhance your exposure and saving money simultaneously.

- Try submitting articles based on the home care world to the small business publications, local paper, newsletters as well as periodicals. Select a topic that interests you and don't forget to give a brief description about home care business. You can also look for a website that would allow you to host a guest column. As soon as you find that your work has been published, ensure making copies followed by delivering them to your potential and current customers.

- There are some professional meeting planners who are always in hunt of workshop leaders and presenters for conferences. Hence, try looking for contact names in the Directory of Meeting Planners or you can also start off with your Rotary Club or Chamber of commerce. If you aren't fond of making presentations then you are free to sign up with your local toastmasters. Believe it or not, but it is considered to be an ideal approach through which you can interact with your potential customers. Whenever you get an opportunity to prepare a presentation, ensure collecting business cards from the attendees.

- You can also start off by introducing an adult education course. This works particularly well for businesses that are service oriented, like the home care industry. Call your local community college or community center where adult education courses are provided.

- One of the ideal ways through which you can get new consumers is by taking help from your already existing customers. Make sure you provide a discount on services to your already existing customers if they have helped you to find new customers. In addition to this, don't forget to send them a thank you note in addition to the discount on services.

- You can also try sending newsletter to your clients. It is important to stay in touch with your present as well as would be customers. Well, in that case a monthly newsletter is sure to help you out. After obtaining permission from the recipients, ensure offering new services, discounts on already existing services, and much more. Try keeping the newsletter simple with chore text. If desired you can also include graphics and photos.

- Every time you carry out anything for a charity like donating free services or materials, or sponsoring an event, be sure the press is aware about it well in advance. They can send a reporter for covering the occasion, however if not, send them images that can be published later on.

- The Internet provides innumerable ways through which you can market your home care business for free. One of the best suited examples of this kind if marketing is through blogging. Through blogging you can create your personal world where your opinion matters. Moreover, the advice you put forward here is of vital importance. Make sure to give your blog an interesting touch as it helps in the effective marketing of your home care business, thereby alluring more and more customers at your door. You can enrich your blog website with logo can colors. You can also invite people to give their opinions on the services offered by them. Interaction with consumers may get interesting and it may be refreshing to see what their opinions are related to your services. you may use this information for improving your offering as well as involving your customers in healthy debate. Blogging may turn out to be addictive, hence avoid spending too much time of your business in blogging. But do not fail to interact with customers as they help in increasing your revenues.

You can also start writing blog or post information to a forum about your home care business. There are innumerable blogging websites through which you can market your home care business. Post any kind of news, promotional messages or information pertaining to your home care business. Another way through which you can market your business is with the help of online discussion groups. Try looking for forums associated with the home care business as well as senior citizen care by entering the keywords at the top ranking online group sites including MSN, Yahoo and Google.

You can also sign up with your local chamber of commerce as well as other community groups as they allow you to interact with business professionals, market your business as well as stay in touch with your community. You may gauge reaction to your product or service in the nearby business community and you may find out the marketing approaches that other business owners adhere to. Getting together with nearby business people will help you create binds which may lead to referral and it will also help in increasing your sphere of influence in your community. You can sign up or rather participate in different events like such as charity fundraisers to help spread your company name as well as increase revenue.

Home care business is termed as a specialized market that needs a combination of assisted living, compassionate care and medical attention. Whether you provide adult day care, hospice services, or long term care, marketing your home care business is important for maintaining high profits as well as patients' levels. The best suited marketing strategies for home care engage in offering outstanding care as well as service options which will be lead to enhanced referrals as well as facility visibility amidst medical personnel.

You don't have to invest a hefty amount to market your home care business. Instead, an effective marketing is one that allows you to blend planned advertising as well as promotional giveaways.

If you are into home care business then make sure you concentrate whole heartedly on this business rather than focusing on too many ventures. Why? Well, for the simple reason that it is often observed that in a fit to sign up with too many ventures, we often fail to accomplish any of the tasks successfully.

Another thing that you need to keep in mind when it comes to carrying out a home care business is that don't involve yourself into this business simply because you want to earn good profits from this business venture. Instead try opting for this venture because you love helping people who are in need of it.

Make sure you create a perfect business plan as it is believed to be the basic pillar through which you can attain success and market your home care business in an effective manner. Don't sway people with your words; instead work on to impress people through your actions.

You can't deny the fact that setting up a home care business is indeed a challenging job, but by putting in adequate efforts, you are sure to get the desired results. Be sure to stay in constant touch with your clients and find out whether they are pleased with your job or not. Of satisfied, they are sure to refer your name as well as home care business to their friends as well as family members. This approach will in a way help you to get more and more clients.

So why look for options, when the benefits of starting off with a home care business are right in front of your eyes!

5 CHAPTER FIVE

A home care business can be categorized under a small business. That means that a home care business owner is certainly a small business owner. When you initially start off with this venture, you may probably have an overall strength of 25 employees or may be even less than that, one office and clients coming in from a single source i.e. only from your own state. But friends, if I am not wrong, then this isn't your aim or rather you may have a secret desire to take your business to the zenith of success. How? Well, in order to run your home care business successfully, you need to have in you the following traits:

- Proper interaction in your community is necessary when you are into this trait. For this, you can initially start off by attending local fairs, civic and business organizations, public meetings to name a few. Be sure to set up speaking engagements for promoting your homecare business
- Make sure you follow-up on any lead that comes your way and don't feel scared for making cold

calls as well as emails. Ensure conducting an adequate research work and consider purchasing suitable phone number/address lists for sending mailers.

- Ensure working on a professional website that helps you to get introduced to adult children, seniors, referral sources and vice versa. As many people prefer opting for online shopping in recent times, make sure that the website you create is at par with the industry.
- Whether you plan for a shared ownership or you want to appoint vendors, work with a financial advisor or local bank or create an alliance with different referral sources, make sure to carry out the needed due diligence

Now, with all these traits in you, you are ready to step into the world of home care business. Check out the following tips that are sure to help you out if you have just started with your home care agency.

- Concentrate on what you do or rather let us say that don't get side-tracked. You need to focus only on your home care business, even if you are running any other business simultaneously. Mixing up too many ventures at a single go will leave you nowhere and restrict your productivity as well as effectiveness. Prefer conducting one thing perfectly instead of doing ten things poorly.
- I guess you haven't started off your home care business simply for saying that "Yes, I have my own business" or rather for making easy cash! Instead you have started off with this venture

simply because you are fond of helping people. If you have built your business using your own skills and talents then you are sure to succeed. So make sure that in addition to creating a profitable business, you need to put in adequate efforts to manage as well as grow it to the fullest.

- Don't hesitate in putting forward your proposal as soon as you come into terms with any potential customer. Make sure to state clearly your mission, goals, as well as service in a crystal clear and not to mention concise manner.

- Don't show as if you known each and everything because that's not possible humanly. Never step behind when it comes to seeking advice from mentors as well as advisors. With their advice you are sure to take your business to a further extent.

- Do your know something...your bank account is believed to be the life-blood of your homecare agency. So it would be advisable on your part to practice as well as perfect the art of being frugal. Keep an eye on every dollar you spend and cross check every expense. Try maintaining a low overhead followed by managing your cash flow efficiently.

- Believe it or not, but there's nothing that can be termed as a perfect business plan. You are sure to turn into a well-formed home care business owner when tested under fire. Don't feel shy when it comes to learn from your mistake and prefer not to repeat your mistakes for the second time

- Entrepreneurship is defined as a lifestyle; please don't mingle it up with 9-5 job. Don't exhaust your owns self as it makes you fall sick, thereby leading you to show less productive in your work. Eat right, continue exercising and devote time for your own self.
- Words often fail to make an impression, so prefer impressing with action and not conversation. Try endorsing your home care business enthusiastically and at the same time tastefully.

The fact cannot be denied that looking for home care clients is indeed a challenging task, hence don't lose clients for reasons that can be prevented. Make sure to take into consideration the following points for keeping home care clients.

- Make sure to put in adequate efforts for investing in your home care business. To be more specific, prefer sending a survey together with your newsletter annually to your clients. Do consult with your clients regarding the quality of the services you provide and ask them what they think about your staff. Ensure taking into account their suggestions that will help you to change your agency as well as services for the better. What I mean to say is that you need to put into practice their suggestions. The bottom line is that when your customers feel heard and valued, they are sure to keep coming back.

- Keep in touch with your clients on a routine basis for finding out whether they are pleased with your staff's performance as well as your jib. If they answer yes, then don't hesitate in asking them for referrals, may be their family member and friend.
- If you come across any problems, be sure to get into the roots of it at the earliest. Avoid allowing them fester or waiting till a family member calls you up! You need to take up the initiative!
- If any of your present clients suggests your homecare agency to somebody else who finally hires your agency, try awarding them or offer them a discount on your services. Ensure sending a thank-you note.

Let us now concentrate on the marketing ideas that you need to take into consideration when it comes to run a home care business.

It is quite likely on your part to come into terms with a cut throat competition while interacting with another home care business. In fact, if you notice carefully, you will find that the United States based home care agencies fight for the dwindling dollar of the customer. So, what are the options that will help you to stand out from the crowd?

- Have you ever wondered how the prospects look for home care agencies? Well, it is quite likely that they would first take the help of any search tool or rather go to any site such as AOL, Yahoo or Google and type in the keywords "home care agency + city and state." That means that you need to have a strong presence on the web so that people can find you as soon as they type in the relevant keywords. You can also opt for the conventional search tools for this purpose, to be more specific you can take the help of Yellow pages, industrial newspapers and directories. These options are believed to be affordable solutions when it comes to marketing your home care business. Magazines that come with sections devoted exclusively to the shopper also show smart search options for advertisers willing to promote their home care business

- Make sure to keep in constant touch with your customers. With the onset of recession, your marketing budget must have shrunk, however this does not mean that you will stop finding good mix of techniques. Believe it or not, but a good mix of technique will help you to maintain a consistent communication with your clients. Try creating a database of customers as well as prospects followed by retaining as well as up-selling them through ongoing communication with the help of direct mail and email.

- Nowadays big motivators to purchase include savings and low prices. Green practices or aligning with a charitable cause may help in keeping your home care business aloof from this competitive market. By concentrating on your caregivers, you can also keep your home care business stand out from the crowd. It would be foolish on your part to show a difference depending on what you are selling, instead you need to concentrate on the ways in which you are selling, who you are as well as the steps you can follows for giving your prospects something new...something unique.

- In times of uncertainty, customers are willing to seek the services of companies who they trust and have faith in. Well, I guess that by this time you have come to know what I am talking about. That's right, I am asking you to make your home care business a reliable one so that people opt for its services without a moment's thought. Now how would you do that? Here we go...
    1. Bring about an improvement in-person sale of your services
    2. go for networking in professional groups as well as business
    3. online social networking

This isn't all, in addition to this; you need to also opt for experimental marketing, for example, the reasons that bring you into direct contact with customers belonging to small groups. Try creating letters which can be customized for following up interpersonal contacts as well as delivering than you notes to the customers.

Positive word of mouth as well as recommendations is indeed of vital importance. Opt for a public relation campaign that is inclusive of quality article placements and reflects your service reviews as well as expertise. Trust me, this helps to make your home care business stand out from the crowd. Another way through which you can create a word of mouth is by establishing an advisory group of clients who would be the first to get updated information pertaining to your agency.

Be sure to create a website that is sure to grab as well as hold prospective clients and help them with the needed information. At the topmost side of your webpage, ensure including information like special pricing, incentives as well as offers. In addition to this, don't forget to incorporate background details about your home care agency, charitable giving, and media coverage and not to mention your own self. Keep aside a separate space where customers are free to share their experiences with the help of a message board as well as post their testimonials and stories.

Be frank in your opinion...did you ever faced a problems while trying to sell your services to a potential client? Well, this is believed to be the most challenging aspect of making a sale. Check out the following home care sale tips that may come to your help.

- You need to first start off by developing a professional greeting. Avoid uttering the common turn "hello" and then straight away jumping into your telephone conversation. Instead try maintaining a formal attitude while greeting your potential customer. What I mean to say is that try being a bit different or rather a bit professional.
- Make sure to introduce yourself together with giving a brief description about your company to your prospective client. However, don't inform about their services straightaway. Make sure that the introduction is general. You can give a hint on the benefits of joining your companies so as to heighten your prospect/prospects curiosity.
- After you have completed your conversation with your prospective client, make sure to end the meeting or the telephonic conversation with a thank you note.

- While making a call, don't forget to inform your prospects about the purpose of making a call. If it is a referral source, be sure to find out whether the prospect you choose is already into a home care agency or not.

- Telephone conversation isn't all when it comes to market a business successfully. So make sure to interact with your customer face to face. What you can do is call up your client and arrange for a meeting. Make sure that the person you choose confirms your meeting schedule. To be more specific, if your meeting is scheduled after two to three days, then ensure sending a letter of confirmation at the earliest. On the flip side, if the meeting is scheduled tomorrow, try sending an e-mail confirmation. Prefer keeping it short but at the same time upbeat.

Who doesn't want to run his home care business effectively? However, despite this fact, we often fail to make our dream of running a home care business run effectively. But with the following ideas you are sure to run your home care business successfully. So, here we go...

Reap the benefits of different phone and computer technology to run your business more efficiently and effectively. Make sure to take into consideration the following points:

- As a small business, you need to have your computers hooked up into a server. They provide reliability and help you to keep a back up of your documents on a routine basis.

- Try replacing your office phone system with a voice over internet protocol system.
- You can buy accounting software which allows you to generate invoices as well as e-mail reminders automatically for late payments.
- You may be having a website for your home care agency, but think twice...does it works in an efficient manner or rather does it help you in alluring potential clients. If yes then its fine but if not then this may lead you into some serious trouble
- Try creating a web based application form and set up an elimination criteria associated with scheduling, educational level as well as salary.
- You may have to devote ample time for creating a schedule for employees. On the flip side, you can save much of your precious time of you opt for software packages. With the help of software packages you can scan for scheduling errors and help you to carry out the calculation of the payroll conveniently.
- Try getting feedback from your clients

When you are into a home care business, you can also hire freelancers for running your home care business successfully. However, prior to opting for this, make sure to take into consideration the following points:

- Try creating a list of your goals, needs as well as skill set needed while hiring a freelancer
- Review job boards together with the rates at which people accept projects
- Make sure to go through the reviews posted by others if you want to appoint freelancers all by

your own self rather than seeking help from a temporary staffing firm
- Make sure to use PayPal as the mode of payment

Now that you have read this article, it is hoped that you have obtained a fair idea on what a home care business is all about and how you can make it all the more successful using the right marketing ideas.

6 CHAPTER SIX

Home care is a term that is related to the services wherein the elder folks do not need to move to the old age homes or care giving centers and instead are provided the same care at their own residence. Home care business is one of the booming businesses in the United States of America. Home care in the US is experiencing such a high because of the rise in the elderly population. According to a recent survey, there are a total of 20,000 home care professionals who are serving the elderly population across the country.

What's the mood in the market?

Well, senior citizens are definitely growing at a much faster rate in the United States of America and going by the pure statistics, you would even find the rate has doubled over the past two decades. Now, the good news is that this growth is going to continue even in the next decade. The people belonging to the age group of 65 and 85 have rapidly increased, thus providing a fillip to the home care business In US. This constant growth in the number of aged people has given a huge boost to the home care givers. The number of people who are getting into this business has also increased manifolds. 7 out of every 10 American have turned old and they are not ready to move out of their residence to some elderly homes and instead would love to be taken care of at their own residence.

Personal home care givers are professionally trained to handle all the needs of the aged and this includes both the medical as well as the non medical home care needs. There are a lot of people who are taking up this business as both the profits and personal satisfaction, associated with this business, is unmatchable. Most of the people associated with this profession have a personal passion towards rendering their services to the elderly. The life expectancy has also increased and this has been possible because of the medical advancements achieved in the recent decades. Nowadays, the senior citizens want to experience an independent living where they are self sufficient in leading their own life without anyone's help. Age may cripple people and thus the need of a professional home care giver has also increased.

Psychologists opine that the seniors who want to stay at their own home are actually well placed in terms of the security and independence. This psychological advantage puts the seniors into good stead than the people who are forced into the old age homes; this is where the personal home care givers score some brownie points over the old age homes. Relocating to a completely new surrounding can not only be very perplexing for the seniors, but also very depressing, so it is often advised that they remain in their own home.

Professional home care services cost mush less than getting the same services from an old age home. Home care business is a little different from the other businesses and here the passion for the job holds much more importance than the money that is offered.

Well, if we discuss about even a decade back, we will hardly find anything about the mass existence of the professional home care services. This has all changed and now we have multiple home care services at almost every city. Choices for the home care services were also restricted due to this reason and the ones that provided consisted mainly of the medial home care. There is a huge problem that is associated with the medical home care services and that is their cost. The costs of all the medical services are much higher than what is charged by the non-medical home care giver. Moreover, the medical home care service professional needs to be a nurse or a nursing assistant to work independently. Above all, the elders have many other needs that may not be satisfied by the medical home care givers.

Now, if we look at the non medical home care givers then there are several advantages associated with hiring their services. The services that are being rendered by these non- medical home care givers are not costly, but are very satisfying for the elderly people. These professionals know that compassion and professional behavior have to be balanced in a proper manner so that the old people feel satisfied with their services. The people who hire the services of the home care givers may have different types of expectations from them, so a home care giver has to live up to the same. Their services not only include the professional care giving, but everything that is related with the daily life of the elderly person.

Now, there are no rigid boundaries for a person to cross in order to establish a personal non-medical home care business. The home care business requires the capability to build an emotional relationship with the clients (in this case the elderly people) and at the same time carrying out all the tasks with extreme professionalism. The earning potential is also very high but your profits may vary with the degree of effort you are putting into your business. There are numerous people who have made a fortune with their professional home care giving business. One thing that holds a lot of importance is the proper marketing of the services. The truth is that there are a lot of home care giving services and one need to differentiate one's business from the others. A proper marketing strategy does exactly the same. You have to find the right marketing strategy that would help you to stand out in the crowd, so that it helps the clients to spot you easily. You have to prove to them the professional capabilities of your business and convey the message that you have the requisite knowledge to provide the best service in the town.

Let us first look at some the prerequisites of becoming a professional home care giver:

You have to have the necessary compassion towards the seniors and need to fulfill all their expectations regarding your service. Well, seniors do have a lot of qualms about the way people conduct themselves and one needs to be really careful about the same.

A professional home care giver tries to make life easier for the seniors by taking the responsibility of all the jobs that have become tougher with age. You have to have the patience and the capability to handle tough situations.

You have to be ready to perform all types of jobs on your client's behalf and that may even include the housekeeping tasks, so you need to be ready for it.

Apart from getting a grip over the above things, the success of one's home care giving business also depends on other factors like the budget, the demographic analysis of your area and finally your marketing strategies. The need for formal training is not necessary in most of the states and one can easily start one's business. It is very important that you find out about the licensing policies pertaining to the state where you wish to establish your business. Your business could be set up on an independent basis i.e. you take care of all the aspects of the business or you can opt to partner with other home care giving agencies like the www.elderhomecarelink.com. You would also have to think about the marketing strategy, which is one of the most important aspects of the home care giving business.

Some of the marketing strategies that would help you to get a strong foothold in the industry are given below:

a) Try to shun going the old way of placing ads in the dailies or magazines. Choose the new methods like providing free e-books, CDs arranging seminars and consultations sessions to spread the word about your services.

b) You can go for the internet marketing way where you would have to market your services over the internet with user of marketing tools like websites and banner ads. Yes, believe me this is the easiest yet the most effective way to tell people about the services. Present statistics reveal that people are more glued o the internet than ever, so use it to your advantage and place the online ads, arrange Webinars and free e-book distribution sessions to market the services that are sought by every 7 out of 10 US citizen.

c) Use the direct messaging service to market your home care services as this is the easiest way to make people aware of your services. The message should be short, yet powerful one liner that can hit the emotions of the recipients and compel them to use your services.

d) Try to analyze the financial status of all the senior clients and you have to provide your quotes based on the same. This is just a marketing strategy where the word of the mouth about your cheap services is bound to spread. You are bound to get more clients through this and is the only way how you are supposed to expand your home care giving business.

e) Try to market your services with Networking- this way you can really make your business popular. There are a lot of people who are into networking and you have to act like a grapevine and stick with them to spread the word of popularity. Try to attend more and more networking events that are somewhat related to your business. Try to find the groups that show interest in your products and better keep a tab on all their activities to remain updated. Networking neither costs a lot nor do you have to put in a lot of effort in order to understand the different technicalities.

f) Lay aside a good sum of money in order to get all your marketing campaigns on time. Thus you can avoid unnecessary delays and carry out the marketing strategies as planned. The timing of the ads, seminars or other forms of marketing is very important as you have to get ahead o eh others in the race (remember, you are not alone in the market and there are many home care agencies functioning in our city.

g) You need to keep on reminding people that you are major player in the market and thus have to take the help of media in broadcasting about your services. Try to place ads in digital as well as the print media. For instance, a timely ad on the radio shows can give you the required publicity. You should not be deterred, if there is no initial response to your ads. This often happens, so do not pull away the ads and keep repeating them from, time to time; it only increases the popularity.

h) The subject of home care giving for the seniors is a sensitive one and every home care giving professional is supposed to understand the sentiments that are attached with it. You have to draw out your ad campaigns so that it touches the various aspects associated with the subject of home care giving while assuring your customers about the facilities and advantages of hiring your services. Present your offer at the end i.e. after you think that you have convinced them with your presentation. This would make them feel that the services are not solely commercial has an element of care attached with them.

i) We all jump to grab things that come for free and this is exactly what you have to do. Try to provide free CDs, seminars and e-books just see the magic! There is bound to be takers of the same and thus you are going to have the free marketing too. The CDs or e-books are a one time investment, so do not worry even if they take a little time and money to produce. You can keep reusing the same and disbursing them to your target audience on a regular basis. This will help to spread the advantages of your services without worrying about the response to the ads that you publish in other mediums.

There is another easier way to enjoy success in this business and that is partnering with the business entities that are already into the field and have an established name. Become a registered partner with reputed home care giving agencies like www.elderhomecarelink.com as they have already done the hard work and all you have to do is carry that forward. Yes, if you are an individual home care giver or an upcoming agency, you can take the help of this agency to work on their behalf. The returns are undoubtedly best and you also do not have to worry about increasing your client base. The marketing and the other aspects related with the business is taken care of by these agencies. There are uncountable advantages of partnering with agencies like www.elderhomecarelink.com and eldercarelink.com.

Non-medical home care giving agencies like Elder Home Care Link www.elderhomecarelink.com and eldercarelink.com are already brand names in the field and they have the necessary infrastructure as well as the resources to help you in your business. This company provides home care services to the elderly people across all the states of the United States of America. The working method of this agency is very professional and they try to analyze the needs of their clients on an individual basis to provide the best possible home care personnel. The home care programs that are opted by this agency do not in any way interrupt the dignity or the privacy of the clients. The home care professionals who work under this company are made aware of all the guidelines that the company has set for its services. This is the only thing that ensures high quality services for all the clients.

Let us find out some of the services that are provided by Elder Home Care Link:

The wide array of home care services include Assisted Living, Adult Day Care, Continuing Care, Geriatric Care Managers, Home Care & Companions (medical and non-medical), Hospice, Nursing Homes, Home Health , Visiting Nurse , Long Term Care Specialists, Durable Medical Equipment , Home Medical Supplies , Live-in Care , Wheelchairs & Scooters, Private Duty Nursing.

Well, partnering with Elder Home Care Link is pretty easy as you do not have to think a lot about pages of documentation and all you have to do is fill up the online business client referral request. Just log on to their site www.elderhomecarelink.com or eldercarelink.com and fill up the business client referral form. The executives of the company would call up to confirm the request and then you would just be a partner of one of the fastest growing home care agencies in the United States of America. Wasn't that easy?

Prior to starting your home care giving business, you should conduct a proper survey of the market condition in your area and find out the demand for your services. If you find that there is adequate opportunity in the market then only get started or you can just partner with the agencies like Elder Home Care Link and choose to play it safe. Other agencies include:

www.eldercareservices.com

www.care.com

www.anitacares.com

www.eldercare.net

www.elder-care-referrals.com

www.cffde.org/**services**/OlderAdults/**elder**online**referral**.aspx

www.choice**seniorservices**.com/

-
-
-

You can simply google 'senior care referrals agencies', then contact them one by one and ask to be placed in the provider list, that way when families call, they can give them your contact. Some agencies may require a fee.

7 CHAPTER SEVEN

Home care business is the new face of the entrepreneurs with a difference! Yes, this new brigade of entrepreneurs is mixing their passion with business and doing this in style. There are a lot of people who are trying their hands at home care business and are not only satisfying the elderly with their services, but are also raking in the moolah. These people are trying to use all the latest technologies like the internet to spread their businesses and believe me they are enjoying every moment of their business. Well, if that is enough to pique your interest in home care business then I would like to elaborate a little more on this business-in-vogue.

To start with, let us learn what this business is all about.

Home care giving is the profession of providing care (both medical and non-medical) to the elderly people. This may include providing medical assistance to help the elderly perform their regular chores. Home care professionals are generally certified nurses who know how to provide assistance to the people who are elderly or terminally ill. There are many people who serve the elderly people across the United States of America in lieu of a specific charge. Most of the people who are engaged in this profession believe in the fact that money is not the only driving factor and a sense of self satisfaction is what gets them going. Yes, home care professionals love the feeling of helping someone especially the people who are not capable of carrying out their tasks in an independently. A sense of worthiness tends to sweep over them and this is considered as the biggest reward that this profession has to offer.

Coming to the business aspect of the home care services we see that this business has a lot of things to offer to the people who want to become a part of it. This is one of the most lucrative business options available and if you think that you have both the passion and zeal to take up a challenging task like providing home care services then this is for you. According to the latest statistics available with us, the home care business is poised to growth exponentially. The reason behind the growth follows from the simple fact that the number of elderly people in the US is also growing at the rate of knots. Statistics reveal that every 7 out of 10 American is turning old and thus are in need of the home care services. The number of people belonging to the age group of 65 to 85 has jumped quite some notches over the past two decades and the baby booming population has turned really old. With age people are getting more and more crippled and the need for help to carry out simple tasks like bathing has turned out to be indispensable. Our hectic schedules and fast paced lifestyles leave us with very less time to spend with the elderly members of our family. All this can be really very depressing for the elders and they feel helpless while coping with regular activities that have got tougher with age. This is the point where the services of the home care professionals seem like a boon from the heaven.

Home care professionals are skilled personnel who know how to take proper care of the elderly people. They have the necessary expertise to handle all the needs of the aged people while taking care not to intrude into their personal lives and choices. This is the most important part of the job of a home care giver i.e. maintaining a fine balance between their services and personal lives. The personal home care giver build a personal camaraderie with their client, but never do they forget that they are professionals who are out there to help. Home care business is experiencing a huge boom due to the sudden increase in the number of old people in the United States of America. More and more people are getting into the business and are creating a huge pool of home care professionals to work across the United States of America.

There are a lot of things that one needs to consider while setting up a home care business. The home care business is generally divided into two types- the medical and non-medical home care business. The medical home care is all about providing medical help to the people who are terminal ill or are recuperating from illness or injury. Generally, the people are not able to carry out their daily activities while requiring regular medical assistance. The medical home care business is much costlier than the non-medical home car. This is because the medical home care requires special medical skills to handle the critical medial situations. It is just the opposite with the non-medical home care; one does not need to have any special skills to handle normal elderly people. They just have to have the patience to hear out the needs of the client and then work accordingly. Thus it is obvious why the cost of this service is lower than the non-medical home care services.

Home care is the most preferred service as it provides the option for the elderly people to remain in their family surrounding, while also getting the support they require to carry out with the daily activities. Most of the elderly people who are shifted to the old age homes find it very difficult to adjust to the situation. The new surroundings as well as the pain of being away from their own home often tends to shit these people into depression thus making life even more tough for them. This is the reason most of the families are now opting for the home care services that are being rendered.

In the United States of America, there are about 20,000 professional home care givers providing their services. This statistics reveals the fact that this noble profession is now being considered by people who want to do something for the veterans of the society and also choose this as a full time career option. The people who opt to turn this profession into a business need to undertake activities like:

a) Creating a pool of skilled home care professionals

b) Arrange the finances to get an office
c) Maintain a database of clients who would be served by the home care professionals
d) Market their services to expand the base from one city to another

Now, this is what one has to start with the home care business and in this the need to market the business is one of the most important aspects. A proper marketing strategy for the home care business is the prerequisite of carrying on smoothly with the business. A concrete marketing strategy will help the business owner to advertise his/her service to the prospective clients across the United States of America. Marketing strategies need to be based on one thing and that is the emotions that are attached with the subject of home care. You need to understand that home care is a sensitive subject for a family and you need to present your offer in a way that they do not get confused with your services. You would have to tell people about the various advantages attached with the home care services. Nowadays, the home care businesses are using the internet as their marketing medium and are trying to advertise their services. Internet is one of the best things that could have happened to modern people. The wide reach of this medium ensures that everyone around the world can get any information they wish.

Internet can also be used to market your home care business and there are a lot of people who are using it effectively to enhance the reach of their business. Internet has a lot of tools like the website based marketing, social networking, forums etc. that can be used to market your service. Let us look at this internet based marketing tools and see how they can be used to advertise about your services.

a) **Website Based Marketing:** Website based marketing is the one is the most important tool to market your home care services. In website based marketing, all you have to do is to try and increasing the number of visitors to your website. For this you would have to increase the page rank on all the search engines. This entails that you learn a little bit about the SEO or search engine optimization technique. This is a technique with the help of which the search engines display the websites that are most relevant to the search keyword typed. Well, if your website rank higher than the others then it is most likely for the internet users to land up on your website. This is a long drawn technique in which you would have to use various types of SEO techniques to increase the traffic to your website. You would have to find new ways on how you can increase the traffic as a higher traffic would mean higher revenue.

You would have to look at the different types of methods that exist to increase the traffic like affiliate marketing. Yes, affiliate marketing has earned a lot of fame as a business model that helped to market products and services. Affiliate marketing can also be used to market your home care business and you need to build a chain of affiliates would market the services on your behalf. The number of visitors who would come to your website after getting a reference from the affiliate would determine their commission. Thus, there are handsome chances of advertising your services to a wider audience. The audience that you determine for your services need to be properly targeted and affiliate marketing does exactly the same. Here you would get hold of the clients who would be in search of such services and yours could just be their choice.

The primary thing about the internet based marketing is that you would have to advertise about your services on a very catchy manner or else there are chances that a visitor would move to some other page. There are millions of websites that are on the same subject, so the internet surfers need to find something interesting to stick to. Thus you would have to provide them all the reasons to stick with your website. Try to present regular articles on our website, so that people get to know various aspects of the home care facilities. You needed to show the sunny side of life as well as your services to your prospective clients. There is all the need to update the articles on a regular basis so that more an more people fall in love with your content want to come back to read more. Thus once your services get famous, you would definitely enjoy a long popularity over the internet.

You also need to learn how to create backlinks to you website so that you would get the maximum traffic. You should lean to post articles in different article directories so that good backlinks are created against the content that you submit.

b) Social Networking sites: The social networking websites can also be used to market your own home care services by building a strong presence in them. You would have to build friends and followers over the social networking sites and try to discuss topics that are related to the home care services. You need to become members of the discussion forums that are around the home care services. There are a lot of people who use the social networking sites to market their home care services effectively. One needs to understand one simple thing; here, you would have to involve more with the people who have elderly people at home and even the elders. This way you can ensure a regular flow of prospective clients to your website. You can paste the link of your website at the end of the comments, so that people feel curious to know about your services and visit your website.

You need to engage people in discussing about the issues that concern the home care ad thus can find the people who are interested in these types of services. Thus it won't be tough for you to get hold of the people to whom you can market your services. This is the most effective way of crating more and more opportunities for people to come to your website. You would have to provide the people real good solutions to their problems whenever issues like home care giving are raised. You would have to keep a good eye on the latest happenings in the industry to provide effective solution. Thus the social networking sites can prove to be a boon in disguise for anyone looking to market their home care services.

c) **Try the distribution of e-books or Webinars-** This is also a real internet based marketing idea where you can create your own e-books and video tutorials to market your services. Your e-book can be based on the various subjects based on the home care business. You would have to discuss in detail and ensure that the book is interesting to read. Now it is time to distribute the same to the people who you feel would like to hire your services. You would need to distribute the e-books through the various social networking sites or through the personal referrals. You would have to gather as much knowledge as possible on the subject that you write your e-books on.

You can also develop-e video tutorials or Webinars to market your services. In fact this is considered to be a very good ploy to entice people into hiring your services. Try to use press releases about the announcement of your Webinars and just see how many people respond to the same. Initially it may be that only a few people respond but do not get deterred. You would have to keep on with your Webinars and ad campaigns till the time you get proper response. In fact there is no reason in closing down your ad campaigns if you get a good response because marketing is a long term game and you would have to keep repeating the same thing again and again. This is just to remain fresh in the memory of your target audience.

Internet based marketing of the home care business can be a great way to reach to the maximum number of target audience. This is not only true for the home care business, but almost all the businesses of the contemporary time. Internet has a wide reach and this act can be exploited to get the best results out of all your marketing campaigns. The marketing strategy for both the medical as well as the non-medical services is the same. The most important element of your marketing campaign is that our campaign should be in alignment with the overall motto of providing the best services in the city. This is one thing that is looked into by all the people who are searching for the home care services.

8 CHAPTER EIGHT

Home care services have come as a big relief for all the people who do not wish to move over to the hospitals or the old age homes. This relief is not only for the people who are worried about their old-aged loved ones, but also for the seniors who do not want to be bereft of the comfort of their home. Over the recent years, the numbers of home care giving professionals have leaped by quite some notches and this rise can be attributed to the fact that the number of senior people in the United States of America has risen considerably. The last few decades have witnessed a phenomenal rise in the elderly population, which in turn has provided a huge boost to the home care business in the United States. Statistics point out that there are a total of 20,000 home care service providers spread over the entire US and the number is continuously increasing.

Home care professionals are the people who provide their care giving services to the elderly citizens. People are more and more attracted to this profession because it not only has its own challenges, but is also one of the most lucrative careers. The best part of being a home care professional is that one has the opportunity to serve the elderly people, which in itself is very satisfying. One can also take up the business of providing the home care services by creating a pool of well trained home care giving professionals. There are already many agencies that are providing this service across the country and helping the old people lead a comfortable life. The market for the home care business is also on a high as the statistics predict a better future for this service oriented industry.

There is great news in store for the people who have decided to embark on the journey of setting up a home care business. The population of the people in the age group of 65 to 85 will keep on rising in the next decade and the need for the home care givers is certainly going to increase. Analyst find that every 6 people out of 10 in the US are in need of a home care professional as they are not physically fit to carry on with their day to day job. The professional home care personnel are trained and have the necessary skills to handle all the needs of the aged people. It has been often seen that the home care professionals develop a personal bonding with their clients. This is something that is treated as the biggest skill of care giver. One needs to understand that this job not only involves professional help, but also has to be blended with compassion and personal care.

The life expectancy of the general citizens has increased over the past few decades due to the progress in medical science. This is the reason why people live longer, but old age does cripple them to an extent that they need the help of someone who can support them in their daily activities. Now, it is not always possible for the family members to take care of their loved ones and the appointment of a home care giver becomes a lot more viable option. The option to shift the elderly to the old age homes is not always preferred because it can be really depressing for the aged people to leave their homes and stay in completely unfamiliar surroundings. The appointment of a home care giver seems to be the feasible as well as the cheapest option in such a scenario.

The elderly people are more inclined towards spending the last days of their lives at their own residence. It is really very confusing as well as depressing for them to live away from their loved ones. It can often act as an element of mental setback for the elderly people and they lose their interest in life itself while suffering from frequent bouts of depression. This can be a real problem for both the family of the concerned elderly person. Now, if the same family members opt for the home care giver then it becomes a lot easier for them to convince the elderly about the idea and even there is also no need of relocating to an old age home. The elderly can be provided the same care at the comfort of their homes. The old people need care and love and both of these can be provided by a personal home care giver who would take care of all the needs and make life a lot easier for the elderly. It has been often witnessed that the appointment of a home care professional has resulted into a better health for the elderly client. Everything is the result o the mental satisfaction of getting care at one's own home.

Coming to the costs attached with the home care giving services then only one thing needs to be said- it doesn't come for free! Yes, it is not free, but definitely not as high as the old age home services. If you are indeed interested in establishing a home care business then you would have to ensure that you are not only aware of the job, but also the other aspects associated with the business. The home care business is the latest money making tool for the entrepreneurs who have both the passion as well as the expertise for providing the services. You need to first understand the requirements of establishing this business. Well, the business requires that you have a pool of well qualified and highly skilled home care professionals. This means that you have to recruit or partner with the people who already have experience in the home care giving business. One thing that you need to understand is that the demand for the home care professionals can be met with the highly skilled workers and you cannot expect to build a team of rookies to rake in the mullah. You have to find the professionals who have the necessary qualification in nursing or who have worked as assistant nurses/nurses at hospitals and care giving centers. You need to check the state laws pertaining to the home care giving services; there are many states where you can carry out your services without any license, but there are also a few who require a valid license for operating the same.

Other than the licensing one of the most important factors is the capital investment- you can either opt to become a virtual service provider or can establish an office. The choice is how you wish to operate your business. For instance, if you just want to work as a home care giving agent then you can set up your website through which you can recruit the home care giving professional and also contact your prospective client. The other option available is to establish an office and conduct all the operation from there. There are a lot of people who are interested in working as an agent as the capital involvement for the same is very less. You would have to just spend in establishing the website and for the internet based marketing of your services. Since we have touched a little on marketing the services, let us look at the methods that you can adapt for marketing your services.

Marketing is the most important aspect associated with a business and home care giving business is no different. You would have to market your home care services in a proper way to increase the number of clients. The increment in the number of client is something that cannot be achieved without a robust marketing strategy. The marketing strategy has to be based on the type of audience that you are targeting and need to appeal to their emotions. A well-structured and properly targeted marketing campaign can yield rich results. In order to sketch a comprehensive marketing strategy one need to first study the market trends prior to designing the marketing strategy. Home care giving is an emotional one, so try to touch the emotions through all your marketing strategies. You need to find something that can provide the right solutions to the problems that the old people are facing. You would have to device a marketing strategy that takes into consideration all the facets of an old person's life.

Home care giving services are basically of two types-the non-medical home care and medical home care. You would have to device two different marketing strategies for them. Medical care giving is generally associated with the care giving for the terminally ill patients or the people who are recuperating from illness. This is mainly for the people who want to get some medical support during the illness. Medical home care services makes it mandatory for a person to possess the necessary licenses for nursing as it involves dealing with clients who are suffering from a medical condition. Medical home care services are lot costlier than the non-medical services. Non-medical services on the other hand are cheaper and even may not require the license to launch the services. It has been often observed that it is very easy to market the medical home care services, but a little tough to market the non-medical one. Let us find out the different marketing strategies that you can adopt in order to gain an upper hand over the other service providers in your area:

Strategy 1) You are marketing a service that is often considered to be an emotional subject, so you have to design your marketing strategy that touches your target clients emotionally. Emotional targeting means that you would have to place your ads on various print and electronic media. Though this is one of the oldest methods of marketing, but still has its own appeal. Since time immemorial people have loved the ads that have come on the radio, television, magazines and dailies. This is the reason you need to place your regular ideas in line and set your ad campaigns on a regular basis. I am emphasizing on the regular ads because there are instances where people pull off the ads just because they do not get the initial response. Now, this is something that can spell doom for your business; you need to have patience and wait for some time before you get your first call. Yes, getting the marketing strategies to yield results is not an easy task and you have to schedule your ads on a regular basis.

Strategy 2) Innovation pays and you can choose to go the off beat way! You are free to experiment with your marketing campaigns and can even introduce your own fresh ways of appealing to people. As we all are aware of the fact that home care giving needs to appeal to both the families as well as the elderly person in question, so you can design innovative presentations for the families. Try to arrange seminars where you would provide insights into the advantages of hiring the services of the home care professional. You need to highlight all the better sides while pointing out to them about the problems that this service can solve. You can even make CD presentation of the same and redistribute the same to the people you know. You can even make your own e-books and distribute it over the internet. Well, this is one of the ideas that seem to work for all. Yes, people love anything that comes for free and if you provide them something like a handbook to know about the home care services then that would only help to spread the word.

Strategy 3) In order to market your services, you can choose the internet as one of you mediums. Internet is the best thing that could have happened to the people who want to market their products or services and you need to use this as your biggest marketing tool. There are a lot of ways by which you can market your services over the internet and some of them are the social networking sites, banner ads, affiliate marketing etc. You can put your banner ads on various websites that would help you to reach the masses. Yes, you are concerned with the ad reaching as many people as possible and there cannot be anything better than the online banners. You can even start your passive marketing campaigns on the social networking sites like Twitter, Facebook, MySpace, Tagged etc. Remember you are going to be banned if you try to market your services directly on the social networking sites, so you would have to keep the sales pitch as low as possible. Try building a relationship with the other members of the networking sites and increase the members. Try to engage people in various types o discussions related to the case of the elderly people. This can seriously result into viral marketing. You can even start with your affiliate marketing campaigns and build as many affiliates as possible. This is really a great idea to market your services to all the other states in the United States of America.

Strategy 4) Use the messaging services to reach out to your audience. Yes, it is better to use the private messaging services to send direct messages describing about your services. Now, there are a lot of advantages of this method and the biggest one is that you can directly reach all your clients. Yes, reaching your ad campaigns or services has become really easy and the clients do not even have to surf through the website to know about your services. The word about your home care services can be really easily spread with the direct messaging campaigns. There are a lot of big companies that use this method and the results of these campaigns have proved direct messaging to be a very efficient marketing tool. Numerous agencies can carry out your direct messaging campaign and all you have to do is outsource your job to them. The regular messaging campaigns are sure to reach as many people as possible thus making it the best weapon in your marketing arsenal.

Strategy 5) Price for your services should be low, so that you are able to beat the competition. This is indeed a good ploy to catch the attention of your prospective clients because it won; take much time for the word to spread. If you provide standard services within a low price range then it can turn out to be your biggest marketing strategy. Your marketing strategy has to be definitely based on the pricing, so that you are able to gain an edge over the other home care businesses.

You can also try out innovative ways to get the attention of our target audience like announcing the insurance claims along with your services or providing special discounts. Now, you need to understand that whatever you do for marketing your services, you would need to make a marketing strategy that would fetch dividends in the long run. Home care services is all about the compassion and services to people who want a little care and you would have to keep these two elements intact throughout your entire marketing campaign.

9 CHAPTER NINE

For a home care company to be successful, they have to have a well framed marketing strategy that will help it reach out to a number of potential clients with success. The home care business is a growing business today and a number of people are opening independent home care centers all over the country. These home care centers cater to those people who are in need of medical and non- medical professional care. They are highly in demand and well respected for the nature of the services they provide. They are an indispensable part of society and they are also helping numerous families all over the country to take care of loved ones. The services of home care businesses are fast catching on not only for their social reasons, but also for their commercial popularity. There are many people who are setting up home care businesses and are earning streamless profits from it.

Today, there are many people in the country who need

recourse to these home care services for looking after the personal and health needs of patients. A home care provider does not only have professional manpower but they recruit people who have the love and the compassion for helping these people with their personal needs. The home care service is undoubtedly very challenging as these professionals need to deal with disabled or elderly people who cannot carry out their daily activities like normal persons. They require the medical as well as non-medical help like feeding, bathing, dressing etc. The home care giver needs to be very friendly and have a caring attitude towards these people. He must be also professionally qualified to deal with normal and urgent situations. There are many individuals who are cranky and suffer from the loss of memory; the home care provider must have compassion and understanding in order to serve these people.

Though the endeavor of being a home care giver is stressful and difficult, it brings a feeling of contentment to persons who are engaged in the profession. People who are care givers feel satisfied to serve society and bring a smile to the faces of those for whom they care. They are responsible citizens who have taken the pledge to do something different for the welfare of their fellow human beings who are now unable to lead active and normal lives. The profession is very challenging and it enhances the self esteem of the person. This is the reason why there are many home care businesses today that are operating and making a difference to society. These organizations not only earn profits, but they are also contributing positively to society with their services.

For those who share the passion of helping others they can set up their own home care business and start operating for the welfare of society. The home care business venture is a very popular and lucrative business venture today. It enables a person to churn out consistent profits every month not only in the terms of money, but also in the eyes of society.

For those who aspire to set up their own home care business venture, they need to take time to plan and execute. The home care business cannot be set up in a day. There are many things that need to be taken into account before one is fully equipped to venture out into the market. The market trends need to be determined correctly. The venture requires a lot of traveling and hence the person needs to be prepared. It is essential to meet people and increase one's network. It is better to equip one with basics nursing knowledge as the venture deals with both medical and non-medical care.

Once the set-up is complete one also needs to focus on equipment and the marketing strategies to create a dedicated customer base. The goodwill and the reputation of the company are very crucial and one must strive to get the highest level of client satisfaction. With increased customer satisfaction the business of a person can grow. Reaching out to the maximum number of people is the main target that these businesses should have. They should make the constant endeavor of providing the best services for the client.

The market trends greatly determine the future of any business. The same philosophy also holds good for the home care businesses too. The marketing tools must be planned according to these market trends and hence the person must conduct an elaborate survey of the market before venturing into the business. In the USA, a person who needs to set up a home care business needs to apply to the State. The application also has a fee that needs to be submitted to the State.

The name of the business and the location of the home care business center are very important for the success of the organization. The marketing is generally based on the above two factors. The size of the home care business will also determine the marketing strategy of the venture. The home care business can be a sole proprietorship, partnership, limited liability company, S Corporation and C corporation. The home care business should be registered with the Secretary Of State and get the Federal Employer Identification Number or the EIN from the IRS.

Once the above has been obtained, a person must also get the required licenses, insurance and the registrations that are required for the business venture. The City or the County license is mandatory for the purpose of legally operating the business in the State. There are some States in the USA that have made it compulsory home care businesses to get the Sales Tax License too. There are 23 States in the country that require the possession of a home care license for a non- medical home based businesses. The applicant must register with the State Revenue Department and in some States one has the option of registering online. The applicant also needs to register with the State Unemployment Service is also compulsory. In addition to this one needs to purchase workers insurance compensation and the business liability compensation.

Once the above has been successfully abide to, the next thing that one needs to go for is a successful business strategy that will help the business reach out to the maximum number of clients. The marketing has to focus on awareness and the generation of needs. It should be remembered that successful marketing includes both compassionate care along with professional services. The marketing plan has to be well crafted and hence needs to be executed with great detail. This is in turn will increase the profits as well as the clients of the business. Be it short-term visits or live in help these home based companies provide increased complementary services in addition with quality based medical facilities.

In order to get the best marketing strategies for the promotion of a home care business, the latter should focus on providing extra facilities in addition to the basic home care services. The home care business can provide home based physical therapy, nutritionist services, counseling and even alternate therapy like acupuncture. If the home based business concentrates on offering a broader spectrum of services it can make draw more customers to its services. The goodwill of the company will increase customer patronage and hence word of mouth and client referrals are enhanced.

In the United States, many patients can get access to home care businesses only on the acceptance of insurance plans. It is therefore, advised for those who won a home care business to accept all many insurance plans in order to increase the customer base of its clientele. The home care business should also offer insurance counseling to its customers so that they understand the terms and the conditions of the plans. The limitations and the benefits of the plan should also be explained to them in detail. If the situation demands, the customers can also be referred to a professional insurance consultant who can make any modifications in the plan as required. In this regard, it must be noted that the insurance representative should be very calm and understanding as most of the clients and their relatives may ask for elaborate details. The patients of home care units are often cranky or they may suffer from memory loss. In the above context it is wise to ensure that the professionals that are counseling patients have a customer oriented attitude along with a friendly disposition. This in turn will prevent negative customer reaction and the professional services of the company can be enhanced too.

Agreements with hospitals, nursing homes, hospital services, diabetes clinics and other medical facilities should also be finalized. The patients are generally elderly people or persons with chronic health conditions. The level of care that is provided to each patient changes and depends upon the condition of the patient. The home care unit should enter into professional agreements between these medical service providers for the transfer of services if and when required. This venture can in turn increase the number of client referrals thus working well for the growth of the business.

The agreements should be well framed and all the terms and conditions should be clear to the parties. Along with the above the home care business should also venture into agreements with expert services in order to get professional consultants and specialists. There is generally a contractual fee that is paid for the above agreements and they are mutually decided upon by two parties. These professional agreements are not legally concerned and hence they focus on quality, accountability and accessibility. These agreements have the positive advantage of establishing a long standing relationship between both parties to the agreement.

The home care business can also use another popular marketing tool in the form of public care. Going the extra mile with home care services can lead to more positive word of mouth and customer referrals. The home care business can in addition to the basic care services also cater to blood care checks, monitoring of blood pressure and flu shot services. This helps the company to project a healthy face and hence serve the people in the community well. There is also another marketing strategy that the home care company can resort to when in business and that is the offering of beneficial services like pet care services, errand running, home cleaning, delivery of food, financial planning, and lawn care services etc. The home care business can provide these services with the help of associated partners. In addition to its business, the health care unit is also promoting the business of these partners and hence can also charge a fraction of the revenues on a contract basis. This in turn leads to providing instant access to other fundamental services related for home care patients.

With regard to the above it now has become evident that marketing is undoubtedly a very important part of any home care business venture. Advertising also has to be done in order to generate awareness and reach out to people who need access to these home care services. The nature of advertising that can be resorted to depends upon the size and the type of home care business that has been set up. There are many modes of advertising and one can adopt all the modes or any one depending upon the nature of his business operations. One can opt for cheap and expensive modes and hence get the best results.

For effective local marketing, one can use fliers to promote the business. These fliers can be distributed in local places like markets, churches, shopping centers, hospitals etc. One can also use business cards that can be kept handy as business opportunities often do come unexpected. One can keep business cards with him and hence produce them when required. The advantage of business cards is when one gives them to another person, he gets referrals that will help him in his business.

The internet is a very convenient and cheap manner to advertise one's business effectively. A good website can be drawn up with vital information on home care services. One can also print articles and write ups relating to the home care business with respective phone numbers and addresses. The net can reach out to a large number of people and hence serves the purpose of being a good and marketing platform. A person can write or publish press releases. Even small email marketing campaigns can promote the business to a very large extent. Adding the home based business to an online directory is also very beneficial. These online marketing campaigns are very popular and they help to increase clients.

The radio is also a very effective advertising medium that the home care business can use for the purpose of marketing. This audio mode of advertising can reach out to a large number of people and hence sensitive topics relating to essential home care services like aging, family relations, childcare etc can be discussed and listeners can get valuable information from them with ease.

The print media is also a very useful media where the person can advertise the home care business successfully. One has the option of advertising in penny savers, community newspapers and area newsletters. Hoardings and billboards at prominent places can also spread awareness about the home care business and thus attract customers to them. There are also places like local health fairs, markets and community sales that one can use for the purpose of advertising and marketing.

There are many marketing strategies that one can use for the successful promotion of one's home care business. These campaigns help the home care businesses reach out to the targeted segment of patients and their relatives. The home care business can also set up a referral program where the patient can get a discount if he is referred to the home care business. Thus, the correct investment in sales and marketing should bring in the best client referrals and inquiries. One must chalk out the plan very minutely. The current market should also be kept in mind and thus the campaigns should be changed as per its demands.

Home care businesses are very lucrative and hence can be taken up as a full time business venture successfully by those who have love and compassion for the old and the sick, These home care businesses employ the services of professionals who both the technical expertise and sensitive mental attributes to serve the disabled and the elderly. This home care business venture is a social and noble venture that not only gives one profits but also respect. More and more people are joining home care units for this purpose and right now there is a very high demand for these services. This profession is very challenging and demands a lot of patience and composure. Dealing with patients can be difficult and one needs to be understanding. The home care giver is a person who deals with the patient compassionately and hence is trusted and respected by everyone in society.

10 CHAPTER TEN

The home care sector is often referred to as "domiciliary care" and involves the health care professional caring for those who cannot look after themselves. They help people carry out their normal daily activities and they are highly respected and trusted in society today. Known as caregivers or voluntary caregivers, they help the patients with eating, dressing, bathing and other daily activities. These caregivers are more of a friend to the patient with their understanding and sensitive nature. The term "home care" is also used to distinguish custodian or non-medical care that is the care that is not provided by nurses, doctors or other registered medical professionals. The home care professional is a person that has a license to provide health care to any person who needs self care.

The professional home care services include medical or psychological assessment, medication teaching, pain management, disease education and management, physical therapy, speech therapy, wound care, and occupational therapy. There are many home care assistance services that provide help with daily tasks like preparing food, administering medicines, laundry, housekeeping, errand running, shopping, companionships and transportation. The home care professionals also help the elderly and the disabled with activities that relate to bathing, dressing, using the toilet, eating and walking. The number of self care professionals is on the rise and they are taking up this highly respected service to mankind as career. There are many agencies that deal with home care services and they employ skilled manpower for catering to the home care needs of millions of elderly and disabled people in the country presently.

The home care sector in the country is divided into two parts and that is formal and informal. The formal home care sector comprises of nurses, therapists, respiratory, occupational therapists, medical social workers, mental health workers etc. The informal sector comprises of the family or the friends of the patient.

Today, home care sector is evolving in a big way as there are more and more people who are taking up home care services as a career. These people are oriented towards the service of elderly people and the disabled. In fact the US Census Bureau in 2008 reported that there are around 8 million Americans who are living with a particular self care disability and more than 17.3 percent of the US population is above the age of 60 in 2008. There are many people who are depending on these services and now they do not opt for institutional care. The prospects of home care businesses, thus, are very bright and so they can be opted for entering into a profitable and lucrative.

The home care sector consists of many motivated, friendly and flexible assistants who are committed to the service of elderly and the disabled. These people combine professionalism along with compassion and sympathy for self care individuals. The home care business is meant for those who love serving others and making a difference to the lives of others with their compassion and love. The past trends, current and future demands are increasing day by day and so this sector can rightly be called a booming sector. It provides consistent monetary returns and a secure future for those who are ready to embrace this challenging but immensely rewarding profession.

The driving force of every home care business is simply love and compassion. This sector is growing at a very encouraging rate. This sector is a very dynamic and diverse industry that provides potential home care business investors ample means to earn and serve society at the same time. It has been estimated that today there are over 20,000 home care providers that are providing home care services to an estimated population of 7.6 million people who are in the need of care because of long term illness, chronic health conditions, permanent disability and permanent illness. Home care services are broadly used to describe a variety of home care related services that are provided in the home environment. It implies the health care that is bought to the home of the patient in order to restore the overall health and well being of the individual.

The non- medical home care providers are successfully providing a rapidly growing trend to allow people that need help in daily activities be in their home or their community.

These home care businesses employ skilled and trained professionals who receive reimbursement from the families of the patient or from other home care providers from whom they have entered into sub contracts for long term health care service.

The growth trends in the home care business are very fast and popular today among most business ventures. The senior citizens are one of the fastest increasing population groups in the USA today. Since the 1980's the senior population has grown twice as fast as the overall population. The growth is expected to double in the next few years and it has been observed that seniors who are above the age of 85 are the fastest growing segments. In relation to this the demand for non medical home care services is also growing. It has been observed that as most Americans grow old they prefer to stay at home. Most Americans also own their own residence and have no plans to move to another place or country. This has led to the rise of home care based businesses that cater to helping these needy people.

In the year 1990, it was observed in the USA that there were 80 per cent of senior individuals who did not have the ability to prepare their own meals at home. They had to take the help of someone for their food. By 2001, the number dropped to 60 per cent. This decrease had resulted due to the number of seniors who reported that they had relatives, spouses, family, neighbors and friends to provide them personal care assistance. It was also psychologically beneficial for these seniors to be in the midst of familiar surroundings. There had been innumerable cases where the seniors had to be sent to retirement homes by their children. This led to depression, isolation and sadness. These negative emotions used to influence them and they fell prey to chronic illness. In addition to this, there was also a marked difference between a senior who needed help with personal care and one who required medical assistance. An elderly person who is relatively healthier when compared to the other adults will not be able to gel with those who are old and infirm. He is bound to feel out of place.

With the advent of home care businesses today the conditions of the senior citizens have improved considerably. Not only do home care businesses cater to senior citizens but they also benefit those who are disabled or suffer from any other physical disability.

The home care businesses employ skilled and trained experts who not only have a compassionate attitude to their patients but they also are the ones who can be relied upon for medical assistance too. These caregivers also enable patients to maintain their independence by taking over daily living activities that become difficult with age. They are also responsible for providing companionship and conversation to these people who feel pampered and wanted by their care givers.

Investing in a home care business is thus a very profitable

venture for the above mentioned reasons. This business venture cannot be set up in one day and this business needs to be entered into carefully and with planning. There should be compelling marketing strategies that will also rake in a steady flow of income as well as serve millions of people who need self care services. There are many platforms for marketing that can be resorted to. The objective of the home care business is not solely for earning profits but for the general welfare of the society as a whole. The marketing strategy of the home care unit is very important for its growth. The market conditions have to be studies and researched and business plans must be set up for operation. A person needs to reach out to a vast number of people and so it is prudent to use the best effective advertising tools to promote the venture.

The most cost effective marketing tool that can be resorted to for the purpose of promoting one's health care unit is the internet. The internet brings with it a host of contacts and is one of the popular advertising mediums today. This medium needs to be utilized in the best possible way and the person who is in charge of the home care business should ensure that there is an informative website on the net. One can provide articles and regular newsletters for the purpose of promotion. There can be forums and interactive chat boards that can enable friends and relatives of self care individuals interact with the health care unit.

The next effective tool that the home care business can invest in is the print media. There can be advertisements in newspapers and magazines that highlight the salient features of the service.

One can also distribute fliers in hospitals, nursing homes, clinics and other relative places where patients and their friends can get access to these services. The radio is also very helpful to promote one's health care services and there can be audio programs on which the health care units can generate awareness on issues relating to personal care. This can be extremely helpful for the patient and his family to know about looking after elderly and disabled people.

For those who have a bigger set up they can use hoardings and billboards that can be put up in prominent locations. These help to spread general awareness and hence make an impact on many clients. Business cards are also helpful as they can be carried easily and handed over whenever the business opportunity arises. This is also very helpful for the purposes spreading business in local circles. This is in turn leads to client referrals that can promote the business in a very big way.

In addition to the basic home care services the home care business can also provide associated personal care additional services to the general public. These services can include physical therapy, nutritionist services, counseling and even alternate therapy like acupuncture. These additional services can be provided at home and the patient does not have to step outside. These diverse services can help the home care business to increase the client base and at the same time spread positive word of mouth. Positive word of mouth thus leads to more customer referrals that can generate a lot of leads for expansion.

Professional agreements with hospitals, nursing homes, hospital services, diabetes clinics and other medical facilities should also be entered into. These agreements enhance the professionalism of the home care unit and thus draw a number of clients to it. The condition of patients change and their subsequent treatment depends on them. In many cases the need may arise for the transfer of services and hence the utility of these professional agreements come in handy.

In the United States many patients can get access to home care businesses only on the acceptance of insurance plans. It is therefore, advised for those who won a home care business to accept all many insurance plans in order to increase the customer base of its clientele. The home care business should also offer insurance counseling to its customers so that they understand the terms and the conditions of the plans. The limitations and the benefits of the plan should also be explained to them in detail. If the situation demands, the customers can also be referred to a professional insurance consultant who can make any modifications in the plan as required. In this regard it must be noted that the insurance representative should be very calm and understanding as most of the clients and their relatives may ask for elaborate details. The patients of home care units are often cranky or they may suffer from memory loss. In the above context it is wise to ensure that the professionals that are counseling patients have a customer oriented attitude along with a friendly disposition. This in turn will prevent negative customer reaction and the professional services of the company can be enhanced too.

Agreements with The patients are generally elderly people or persons with chronic health conditions. The level of care that is provided to each patient changes and depends upon the condition of the patient. The home care unit should enter into professional agreements between these medical service providers for the transfer of services if and when required. This venture can in turn increase the number of client referrals thus working well for the growth of the business. These agreements are entered into a contractual basis and a specific fee is paid. The sum of the fee depends upon on the mutual agreement. In this way the business benefits and both of the parties to the partnership can earn revenue. This marketing tool also helps the patients and the relatives to rely on the home care units for their loved ones. These agreements enhance the professionalism of the home care unit.

Another marketing tool that a person should keep in mind is to accept insurance plans. In the United States of America there are many patients who can only get access to home care businesses only on the basis of insurance plans. It is mandatory for all home care businesses to accept as many insurance plans for a successful and effective long term inflow of clients. The home care business should also have the services of an experienced insurance counselor who can make the patient and his relatives understand the terms and conditions of an insurance plan. The person should be sensitive and understanding as he is dealing with people related to the elderly and the disabled. In this regard the person should be patient and not lose his temper. This also prevents negative reactions and the home unit can earn a good reputation. These services can also be further enhanced if the home unit keeps a professional insurance adviser for the purpose of any kind of any modifications in the insurance plans. They also can help people understand the various limitations and benefits of a plan and thus contribute positively to the home unit's growth.

It must be remembered that the correct marketing resources must be used in order to get the maximum effects. The advertising tools can be used together or used separately in order to get the best market effects. A detailed research and survey should be carried out and then the advertising tool should be selected. The objective is to reach out to the maximum people with the minimum efforts. One must either adopt all or some of the above marketing strategies to get the best client and customer response. The home care business is very popular today and it is the ideal venture for those who wish to bring a smile to the faces of thousands of persons who need personal care services.

11 CHAPTER ELEVEN

OTHER WAYS OF MARKETING HOMECARE BUSINESS

How to Market Your Home Care Business by Remodeling

Revamping a house may be done either for esthetic purposes or out of necessity, however whatever the case it is a move that could help increase the viability of a business thus increasing financial returns. Remodeling greatly improves the look of a house and gives a good impression to potential customers, most of whom would like to be associated with a respectable looking enterprise.

When promoting a particular business, the use of visual marketing materials such as brochures, websites and fliers is necessary and a visual representation of the product on offer will have to appear on them. In the case of a home care business, the main focus of attention is the premises where the services are offered. An attractive building will reflect well on the company promotional material and this will help market it as a credible establishment.

A newly remodeled home care premises is bound to have modern equipment that can be used to market the establishment as a state of the art facility and this makes it much more attractive to potential clientele. Visitors and clients to the premises are sure to be impressed by the appearance of an improved building structure and they could inadvertently become marketers for the business by mentioning it to other people. Remodeling could also include some enlargement of a property and this means that the business capacity can be significantly improved.

Reports from realtor groups have shown that although remodeling requires a significant amount of money, the activity of home improvement greatly increases the value of a property. The revamping of a property ends up improving the surrounding community and makes an area more favorable for business. This will mean that prospective clients will consider the location to be favorable.

The home care business is likely to get sufficient tax breaks accrued from expenditures incurred during the process of remodeling. The amount that is exempt could be channeled toward the marketing of the business and other promotional activities. The amount that is exempt by the tax department will however depend on whether the job done on a property is a major rehabilitation or just a minor fix up. Home care ventures sometimes require specialized equipment as well as additional fittings and in many cases there is a need for some amount of renovation in order to make room for these additions. This will increase the appeal of the home care business and give it more marketability.

Although it may not be considered by many home care business owners to be worthwhile, the structured revamping of a housing property can go a long way in creating a business environment that is favorable for growth. Apart from improving the esthetics and getting extra fittings, additional security and safety features can be added to the building and this will act as a selling point for the business. All home business owners who intend to use remodeling as a marketing method should first carry out a thorough research before embarking on this intensive but viable activity.

Using Your Own Book To Market Your Home Care Business

The homecare business in United States is becoming an attractive home business venture for many business minded individuals. This is partly due to the fact that the seniors group is growing at a much faster rate compared to other demographics. With this growth expected to increase further, the possibilities of coming up with both a profitable and a caring service is high. According to statistics, the number of home care givers that operate in the country stand at around 20,000 who provide services to more than 7 million families. Such services range from offering quality care to individuals with acute illness, terminal illness, and long-term conditions among other illnesses. With this high number of home care providers, getting a slice of the market can prove difficult unless the right marketing strategies are effectively used. One of the strategy that has proven successful in other markets and can be used in marketing a home care business is coming up with a book that more or less deals with services provided by the home care.

Market savvy entrepreneurs have identified the role a book can play as a decisive marketing tool. Other than providing new and much better income to the home care business, writing a book related to the home care business will make the homecare business appear professional and increase the owners marketing influence. This is because the book will be read by different clientele who will not probably have heard about the business through other advertising medium. However, before the process of writing, homecare givers or owners must keep in mind that not all books will sell. For the book to sell and achieve its target of marketing the home care business, it has to be aimed at a particular group. This means it must concentrate on a single topic or two or more related topics. Home care business owners need to write books that only deal with provision of home care services and its relevance in today's society.

When writing the book, the first step that must be adhered to is identifying the need that is lacking in the society. In this case, provision of care to the elderly is what is missing. The home care book should be able to provide a solution that will solve the above problem in the lives of the readers. Once the missing need has been identified, the next step is to inform the readers on the steps they can take to satisfy that need. It is prudent to identify all the essential steps readers ought to take to solve their problem. The steps given should be able to provide the readers with ways of moving them from where they are to where they want to go. To make the book digestible and easy to read, every step should be divided into sub steps that can then be used to form complete book chapters.

When all the steps have been identified, home care owner needs to identify the advantages or benefits that the target market will receive if they put what is written in the book into action. The book should clearly indicate the goals that will be gained by the readers once they have read and put the book into use. Identify how the lives of the target market will improve once they start to use the services identified in the book. The home care owner should provide as much benefits as possible since these benefits will be what will attract the readers to using the product or service. Once the book has been completed, consider giving out free copies or autograph each copy before selling them.

Using Mail-Out Newsletters To Market a Homecare Business

Majority of people most specifically the elderly have a bring problem when it comes to them leaving their houses. Basically, this means that they are not able to access the care they require when they most need it. People who are concerned in situations like this will hire professionals to come and take care of such kinds of people from their homes. These professionals are trained to assist the elderly or sick with the tasks, which they are not able to perform and do what they need to do the most. A homecare business will give you the opportunity to assist these people and at the same time be able to earn a living while you are at it. News letters are an ideal way to keep in touch with your patients and potential clients.

Over the years newsletters have gained popularity as being a well established and widely distributed email marketing strategy. They are used by many online, home and company businesses. The newsletters are usually filled with useful information concerning services and products provided by the business. A newsletter offers a way for websites and home care businesses to make a connection with potential and existing customers. They come in handy for customers since they are given the opportunity to read through them at the time they deem fit and are simple for most home care businesses since they are able to send them to many people all at once or they can be set as automated reply.

A home care business newsletter offers the opportunity for you to inform subscribers about the latest happenings on your homecare business. On the other hand, it allows customers to get in touch with your homecare business and let them know about the entire industry for those with no idea what home care is all about. It is of great importance to maintain contact with your existing and potential customers and mail out newsletters will assist you in doing that. After you have gotten permission from recipients, it gives you the ability to offer services that are new, provide discounts to the existing customers, profile a customer or employees, incorporate an advice column on your own and many other features.

In today's world, people have no time to waste reading complicated stuff. The newsletter should be kept simple using graphics, photos and texts. Even though elegant graphics are wonderful, do not lose focus on the fact that news letters are concerned with news, thus limit your information to relevant news concerning home care and the elderly. The text should be boldly presented so that it can be easy to read. You can also use bullet points and short headlines to get the point out fast. An ideal home care business letter should be informative. Since you are the home care expert, you should be able to lay out what you do in such a way that your readers can use the information you give them to their advantage and to answer all the questions they may be having concerning your home care business.

Using Link Exchange to Market a Homecare Business

Many business providers who own home care businesses encounter some difficulties when formulating marketing strategies that can generate overnight returns. The traditional marketing strategies are effective though relatively costly; these methods include television, newspaper, magazines and journals. In case you are a small scale home care business owner, these options might be rather costly. Therefore, the internet has created an enabling platform for home care business owners to effectively market the services they provide. Apart from link exchange, there are quite a number of marketing strategies that people can use to generate more cash. You can have access to information within your surrounding that might be of great help to you as you market your home care business.

Using the most recent innovation is an example of an outstanding way of marketing your home care business. Advertising through link exchange is not only an affordable marketing strategy; it also yields best results. Link exchange is part of the commonly used marketing strategies by business owners. Exchanging portal links with different sites that have similar items related to your services or products aids in attracting the attention of the client. It massively boosts your home care's website popularity, which comes in handy as you try to enhance the rankings in various search engines. Several well-known search engines offer home care business owners with amazing site rankings that make use of link exchange as they market their businesses.

Link exchange does not just market a home care business, but also boosts the visibility of the site. Consequently, the improved visibility leads to more visits and more clients.

Publishing sites directly in online directories can catch the attention of many potential clients as well. Clients use several online directories to look for sites that offer services and products that suit their tastes and preferences. Normally, these directories arrange websites according to the products they offer. This helps clients find sites that offer particular products, whereas the online directories offer substantial number of trustworthy clients. Posting quality content that is related to your home care business is the best approach to use if you want to maintain all your clients.

A dedicated product portal makes it possible for clients to make any purchases directly from you. On the other hand, owners of home care businesses need to be careful while posting images due to the fact that several images in the website are copyrighted. That is the main reason why entrepreneurs specializing in home care businesses appoint experts to create their sites. Increasing awareness of your home care business using link exchange will pay you back with plenty of cash.

You can also decide to send articles that have a strong connection to your home care business and incorporate your business link to different online sources. In return, these firms will submit the articles in various journals and publications. All these home care business marketing tips using link exchange will present home care owners with affordable means of marketing their business and increasing the number of clients they serve.

Using Internet Referrals To Market Your Home Care Business

With the rapid increase in the use of the internet in the world today, there has been a revolution in the way businesses conduct their activities. There has been a shift from the traditional ways of promoting businesses to the more internet based strategies. However, referrals; be it online or through individuals still remain a popular way of marketing a business. The success of the business is highly dependent on the degree in which customers refer the business to other people. Attraction of new customers to a business is time consuming and expensive if left to the customers only.

Internet allows home care owners to promote their businesses to potential customers who in turn are enabled to refer the business to friends, family as well as colleagues. The following are some of the internet based referrals that can be used.

- **E-mail newsletters**. This involves the inclusion of valuable incentives as well as useful content in newsletters that are sent through e-mails. These incentives are supposed to encourage clients to forward the newsletters to potential customers.
- **Promotions.** Giving of offers and discounts to already existing clients to bring in new customers to the business is the other method that is widely used.
- **Unique website features.** The inclusion of extra features that will make a website self-sufficient will increase the amount of customers since the features acts as an attraction.
- **Features for emailing friends.** Websites that have this feature simplifies things for visitors to the site who will be able to send emails with information or content to people who might be interested.

Internet referral site such as elderhomecarelink.com is the finest referral source dealing with business offering non-medical care to seniors. It is a referral company that is internet based and was set up with the aim of assisting clients to live a high quality life for as long as possible. They comprehend that a solitary solution does not suit each and every situation. They take time to learn the preferences and needs of every client by listening to each one at a time. This enables them to refer clients to reputable home care service providers who guarantee to uphold the dignity and independence of the client.

All the information is reviewed to assist in the placement of the client in the most suitable home care provider that will look after the client in the best possible way in addition to meeting their specific needs. At present, the agencies specializing in homecare within their network provide services such as medical and non-medical home care, private nursing, companion care, residential home based facility living as well as adult day care.

Internet referral websites are designed to meet specific needs of clients, be it an individual or a home care business looking for clients. The first point in benefiting from the marketing services provided by the referral sites is to first visit the website. Using the website will allow your home care business to get a wide client exposure and in the end increase your clients and profit margin.

Using Free Give Away Items To Market Your Home Care Business

Any business would require a good advertising plan which is its main strategy to achieving great success. With a good marketing strategy, word will get out to your community and people will know that you are providing certain products or services. So without a good selling plan, your business will be slow and it will definitely affect your income capabilities. This is not any different if you are operating a home care business, because the local community still has to know the services you are offering. Marketing enables them to know if they will prefer your home care business over your rivals.

It is quite difficult to penetrate the market because of the stiff competition between businesses and brands. It is almost impossible for a small business to gain a top edge over established businesses. It is very difficult to catch the attention of the public with no voice and a tight budget. However, small businesses have made it big as well with little budget and great efforts. The most important thing in marketing is creativity and persistence. Most home businesses make use of a strategy that is disregarded by some big companies nowadays and this is free give away items.

Free give away items are great for small home care businesses that seek to gain an edge in the market. Give away items can be handed out in many events to potential customers. These events include promotional tours, exhibits and conventions. In most cases, business owners give away product samples. For instance, if your home care business also involves food products, you can go to schools and promote your product by giving out samples of your products to schools kids; if kids love the product, they will ask their parents about it. You can also offer free testing samples in supermarkets or give away a packaged sample to clients.

Furthermore, business exhibits and conventions can be the perfect place to issue free giveaway items such as key chains, mugs, pens and many more. Although these items may not belong to your company, they have to carry your brand name and logo that potential customers can take home. Giving away such items may seem like a small thing but at the end of the day it is the most important part of the marketing strategy. Despite the fact that not all onlookers are your potential clients, they are the still the same people who will spread around news about your home care services.

For companies that you do business with, it is still important that you strengthen the business ties with them, even though you have been in business with them for years. Keep sending them giveaways, not just because they help promote your services and you earned great profits but to maintain that business relationship. Moreover, it is advisable to keep in touch with them especially during holiday seasons and create an impression that the business relationship is still there. Keep in mind that there is a possibility that those past clients are the same people who will recommend you to other people who may need your services. Past clients will always remember you from the pens and mugs sent to them with your home care business name or logo.

Take Advantage of Online Video Marketing To Increase Your Home Care Business Clientele

Viral marketing is known as word of mouth in offline business, whereas online business is also referred to as viral marketing. Though many have tried to rename this term, viral marketing is still the name that most internet users acknowledge and recognize. Furthermore, it is very advantageous in business to act like a real virus though in constructive way. When promoting your business, you definitely go to different places and this way, you behave like a virus by spreading to different blogs and sites as you try to set links to increase traffic in your website.

You can take advantage of online video for your home care business to gain traffic. Use text-based blogs, articles and video blogs that can really attract audience to view your site or weblog. Moreover, internet users and online marketers can share stories, opinions and commentaries in online video, where you can incorporate video clips, images, special effects and stories concerning the services provided by the home care. Here are some tips on how you can take advantage of online video to increase your home care business clientele:

First you have to decide on the best topic for your online video. Select a niche title that will highlight what your video is about. That is the reason why it is more appropriate to select a topic that is correlated to your business. For instance, if your home care business also involves providing health care products to the elderly, you can offer tips in skin and face care, ways of maintaining a healthy skin and foods to be eaten to maintain a healthy skin. An attractive and relevant niche title will easily attract prospective customers to stop over your company website or blog and this will increase traffic and possible clients to your business.

If you thought that pictures have a greater impact then you are wrong because videos have much more. So make use of quality video clips, music and images in the online videos. You should mostly invest in good videos for your website because videos that are professionally and creatively done have a high chance of attracting more internet users. Moreover, keep in mind that your business will be reflected by the type of videos you make. This is the reason why you should use great video clips, images and even music to make your marketing campaign a hit.

You can also speak to your clients directly since online video marketing are intended to elicit emotions apart from communicating to the audience. This is why it is important that you make videos that speak to your customers through a personal approach or tone. You can also include links in your home care marketing video to enable viewers click the specific page. The best way to incorporate these links is by placing them randomly on your video because this will draw the user's attention to view your home care's website. Other bloggers use links for the purpose of recall and this can also draw potential clients to your website. Furthermore, register with free video hosting websites and you will be able to upload free videos.

With this, your business can upload videos that could be used to market certain products and services and will draw clients to visit your home care business site.

Marketing Your Home Care Business Using the Internet

Being the owner of a home care business can be very fulfilling; the idea of offering home based support for various individuals is noble and can as well lead to great profits. In this type of business, the use of internet can offer numerous marketing platforms that are important for generating awareness of the services being offered, thus attracting potential clients. There are several ways of ensuring that online presence creates an impact for any business.

The first step should be to conceptualize and develop a custom website. This could either be done personally or with the help of a web design specialist. Web designers normally create the site from scratch and could either maintain it for the client or give the appropriate instructions to the site owner. Whoever designs the site should come up with a simple and practical site that focuses on the home care business and the services that are offered.

The site has to be easily navigable for ease of use. The site should include the company's, general information, business portfolio, services, contact information, and testimonials. Home care is a service; therefore the use of customer testimonials will give more credibility to the establishment and help in creating more awareness of the services being provided. The inclusion of photographs will further enhance the appeal of the website.

Creating a blog is a good way of marketing a home care business and it should be regularly updated for the sake of avid readers. Blogs normally generate a large following and through the large viewership, a potentially large market base can be tapped. The blog should be appropriately linked with the official website to make it easier for potential clients who need additional information. It is guaranteed that a section of the blog or website browsers will actually require the service and without an online presence it would be difficult to tap the market.

Online advertising has become a massive industry and business people are advised to use them as promotional marketing tools. The most recommended type would be pay-per-click adverts that are only paid according to the number of times an advert has been clicked on. By doing this, one can use popular search engines as well as popular social networking websites that all have a great amount of web traffic.

The internet is very versatile and today one can view videos and listen to audio podcasts online. Generating audio or video content is an interactive way of communicating with prospective consumers. This method of promotion is very persuasive in addition to being insightful.

Linking the official home care business website with other similar sites is a good way of increasing web traffic, thus reaching more potential customers. This could also lead to partnerships with like-minded entrepreneurs. The opportunities on the internet are virtually limitless and it is hard to ignore the amount of people that can be reached. It is for this reason that home care business owners are highly advised to use the internet to fulfill their marketing objectives.

How To Market Your Home Care Business Through Networking

Marketing is the most outstanding way of making your home care business known. Marketing options usually vary from exceedingly affordable such as distribution of flyers to excessively costly plans that involve purchasing advertising space in local newspapers. On the other hand, networking is vital to any kind of home care business. The most outstanding way of networking is using your current clients. Come up with referral programs that offer realistic home care discounts or gifts to customers if they refer new clients to you. The marketing tactic possibilities are infinite and are specifically limited by someone's originality. That is why you need to exercise patience and with time, you will eventually get plenty of customers.

There are many networking options that owners can use to advertise their home care businesses. An example is taking photographs. When you are marketing online, you will not benefit from showing clients your services personally because you will have to use text and photographs. Due to the fact that photos are an important way of selling online products, owners might decide to invest in photography to capture their home care business. This will work better if you take the pictures yourself. However, marketers must ensure that their lighting is good and natural as well. This means that home care owners must take photos that will bring out the beauty of the home and which can be offered to clients who can in turn give them to friends and colleagues.

Joining marketing forums is the best way of networking with

other home care business owners interested in expanding their business. This way, you have more opportunity of sharing advice, skills and increasing your popularity with other related businesses. When talking with other people in forums, avoid advertising your home care business within your posts. Marketers can generate links to your blogs or whichever sites that function using your signature.

Care providers who want to market their home care businesses can decide to start up blogs. If you repeatedly update your blog, you will give new viewers a better chance of generating more interest in your business. The blog ought to be somehow related to make your clients interested in your services. This means that you need to start sharing your ideas and make all the necessary reviews on the things available in the home care businesses. Although quite a number of the people who visit your site might not be attracted, you are assured of getting more business from the few people who are interested.

In case you plan on successfully marketing your home care business through networking or increasing it popularity, you have to be very watchful when making considerations to your tastes and preferences. You need to make all the necessary research on methods you plan to implement. Furthermore, it is important that you follow your passion prior to making up your mind on what you need to do with your home care business. Networking will present you with a wide market of potential home care clients, thus you need to develop ways of attracting and maintaining clients who have shown interest in your business.

How To Use Social Networking To Market Your Home Care Business

Social sites for networking are not only meant for the young people to make a connection with their age mates. Today a number of social sites exist that are developed for the sole purpose of business. Some other sites cannot distinguish markets instead they offer online services where business and personal related profiles are available side by side. These sites offer opportunities in which home care businesses can get exposure and be able to advertise their services and products. They can also network with existing and potential suppliers as well as customers. At the same time the home care business can be able to recruit partners and employees to strengthen its performance.

Social sites like Facebook, MySpace and Squidoo are essential for marketing home care businesses. They make it possible for you to introduce your homecare business to a large crowd of potential clients as long as you are able to use them appropriately. The first thing you should do to market your home care business through the social sites is for you to work on your profile. The profile is one way of telling the world about you and your business and if there is a website, clients can be directed to it. The importance of social networking is that it allows you to introduce the business to the entire world. You should therefore ensure that the profile has valuable content making it able to sell the business to the world.

Spend some time to visit the pages and profiles of other site members. As often as it is possible, leave comments. It is important to keep your statements respectful and polite, since people will always be able to trace you through the networking page. You will be able to receive many back links and comments through this way and your profile will be able to appear on the search engine results and this brings in more traffic to your social site.

Majority of social networking sites have groups, which you can join so that your profile can be highly ranked. It is important for you to join a group that has similar interests to the services provided by the home care business. One way to ensure that people keep coming back to your site is by regularly providing interesting stuff. This can be in the form of reports, downloads, e-books that in some way should reflect what your homecare business is about.

Social networking for your home care business can also be done offline. You can spread word about your business by mouth. This can be done by encouraging more people to create their own profile pages and link it to your profile page, thereby generating more interest and traffic for you. Ask people to invite their relatives and friends to join the revolution of networking despite the fact that only a handful can actually link back to your home care business and in turn your sales and traffic will be multiplied. Social networking goes a long way in ensuring your home care business is properly marketed and in turn brings in more clients and revenue.

How to Market Your Home Care Business by Remodeling

Revamping a house may be done either for esthetic purposes or out of necessity, however whatever the case it is a move that could help increase the viability of a business thus increasing financial returns. Remodeling greatly improves the look of a house and gives a good impression to potential customers, most of whom would like to be associated with a respectable looking enterprise.

When promoting a particular business, the use of visual marketing materials such as brochures, websites and fliers is necessary and a visual representation of the product on offer will have to appear on them. In the case of a home care business, the main focus of attention is the premises where the services are offered. An attractive building will reflect well on the company promotional material and this will help market it as a credible establishment.

A newly remodeled home care premises is bound to have modern equipment that can be used to market the establishment as a state of the art facility and this makes it much more attractive to potential clientele. Visitors and clients to the premises are sure to be impressed by the appearance of an improved building structure and they could inadvertently become marketers for the business by mentioning it to other people. Remodeling could also include some enlargement of a property and this means that the business capacity can be significantly improved.

Reports from realtor groups have shown that although remodeling requires a significant amount of money, the activity of home improvement greatly increases the value of a property. The revamping of a property ends up improving the surrounding community and makes an area more favorable for business. This will mean that prospective clients will consider the location to be favorable.

The home care business is likely to get sufficient tax breaks accrued from expenditures incurred during the process of remodeling. The amount that is exempt could be channeled toward the marketing of the business and other promotional activities. The amount that is exempt by the tax department will however depend on whether the job done on a property is a major rehabilitation or just a minor fix up. Home care ventures sometimes require specialized equipment as well as additional fittings and in many cases there is a need for some amount of renovation in order to make room for these additions. This will increase the appeal of the home care business and give it more marketability.

Although it may not be considered by many home care business owners to be worthwhile, the structured revamping of a housing property can go a long way in creating a business environment that is favorable for growth. Apart from improving the esthetics and getting extra fittings, additional security and safety features can be added to the building and this will act as a selling point for the business. All home business owners who intend to use remodeling as a marketing method should first carry out a thorough research before embarking on this intensive but viable activity.

How To Capitalize On Word Of Mouth To Promote Your Home Care Business

There are very many ways of marketing any kind of business in the world today. The methods of promotion vary from the most sophisticated methods to the least sophisticated of them all. The effectiveness of each type of promotion method depends on the type of industry and business that one is running. In home care business, word-of-mouth can be an effective way of promoting the services offered.

Promoting the services through word of mouth is basically the spread of information to customers through speaking to them and they in turn convey the same information to their friends and colleagues. For the business to make effective use of this promotion tactic, there are a number of strategies that can be used to achieve an effective campaign. They include the following:

Tapping Into the Existing Social Networks

Although many people believe that word of mouth involves only speaking, the use of internet has changed this. The user groups in many of the social networks can assist in increasing a product's brand awareness. Using leverage as well as tapping into the social networks with content and tools targeting a particular sub culture will likely draw lots of attention. Some of these comprise of application targeting websites with specific platforms such as Firefox, Facebook and Wordpress, which boast of large number of users. The content that mentions, examines and analyzes sites in large niche might work as well.

Targeting the Main Influencers

Search for individuals or authorities who set trends in relation to a particular topic. They are normally the people who have lots of personal connections, a loyal and large audience. Promotional messages sent by these people in relation to your home care business will be disseminated to potential users in the target group.

Identify the influencers, create a relationship and then market the products by means of the social influence sphere that they already have. The influencers can comprise of influential people in the community, celebrities and even ordinary people.

Scarcity and Exclusivity

Exclusivity generally evokes curiosity while scarcity of products evokes conversation and demand that is consistent. When the demand and conversation are evoked from potential customers, then the work of the influencer begins as they will try as much as they can to promote the business. In addition to influencer's marketing, the home care business will have an outstanding way of disseminating brand awareness and knowledge for new services and products provided.

Micro-Marketing

Micro-marketing normally focuses on promoting the products to an individual through provision of products that are highly customizable. This is in contrast with viral marketing that leverages web interconnections to disseminate promotional schemes that are user-supported or spreading of unique content. A combination between scarcity, social networks and micro-marketing can generate exposure through the word-of-mouth.

Industry Marketing

Focusing on individuals who are responsible for the creation of brands is recommended as opposed to focusing on customers directly. Establishment of relationships and connections that are leverage able is the path that the business should adopt as opposed to looking for numerous views from large audiences.

Looking for recommendations from other similar businesses in the industry, which are to be promoted, mentioned and included in the recommendations ranking list is recommended. This develops the overall brand in a particular niche and in turn it promotes the site you developed to conventional buyers to the business.

ABOUT THE AUTHOR

Jane John-Nwankwo is a Registered Nurse who loves to write. She has authored more than 20 books ranging from Textbooks to Exam Preparation materials, and now to fiction which is termed "Nurses' Romance Series"

Simply search
"Books by Jane John-Nwankwo"
On Amazon.com

Visit her website:
www.janejohn-nwankwo.com

Have you bought this book?

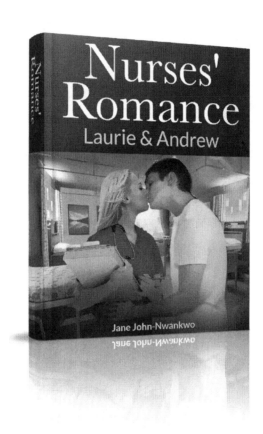

Visit www.janejohn-nwankwo.com

Have you purchased these books?

Made in the USA
Middletown, DE
20 January 2017